THE ASTROLOGY FIX

Brimming with creative inspiration, how-to projects and useful information to enrich your everyday life, Quarto Knows is a favourite destination for those pursuing their interests and passions. Visit our site and dig deeper with our books into your area of interest: Quarto Creates, Quarto Cooks, Quarto Homes, Quarto Lives, Quarto Drives, Quarto Explores, Quarto Gifts, or Quarto Kids.

First published in 2020 by White Lion Publishing,
an imprint of The Quarto Group.
The Old Brewery, 6 Blundell Street
London, N7 9BH,
United Kingdom
T (0)20 7700 6700
www.QuartoKnows.com

Text © 2020 Theresa Cheung
Illustrations © 2020 Alessandro Cripsta

ISBN 978 0 71125 525 8
Ebook ISBN 978 0 71125 526 5
10 9 8 7 6 5 4 3 2 1

Design by Rosamund Bird
Printed in China

MIX
Paper from responsible sources
FSC® C016973

THE
ASTROLOGY
FIX

A Modern Guide to Cosmic Self Care

THERESA CHEUNG

Illustrations by Alessandro Cripsta

WHITE LION
PUBLISHING

CONTENTS

Introduction

Throughout time, people have relied on the wisdom of astrology to help them understand their past, empower their present and create a fulfilling future. By harnessing the power of the stars and planets that you were born under, you can gain a profound understanding of yourself and your life.

My mother was a professional astrologer and often talked of the guiding power of the cosmos, so from an early age I understood that astrology could be an amazing tool for personal growth and development. I was a sensitive, rather shy child, but my astrological insight gave me the confidence to understand both myself and others better. Indeed, knowing the magical potential of the day on which someone was born proved so pivotal for me that I went on to write the bestselling *Encyclopaedia of Birthdays*. Since then, I have continued to explore the power of the universe and how it inspires understanding of ourselves, most recently in *The Moon Fix*, a collection of 48 practices that enable you to harness lunar energy for personal growth and development. *The Astrology Fix* provides a complementary set of resources centred on the stars and planets linked to your own birth chart and I hope it will have a similar transformative effect.

The astrology fixes in this book aim to open up your self-awareness, showcase your strengths and demonstrate how you can become the best possible version of yourself. But they also shine a light on your shadow side, or the areas you need to work on to help you deal with challenges and evolve in the process. All the fixes here are simple and practical, and you can easily apply them to your daily life. You'll learn how to attract joy and success, and how the stars and planets impact your love life, your relationships, your choice of career and your health and well-being. No prior knowledge of astrology is required to work through this book. But by the end you will have enough awareness of your unique astrological blueprint not to only know yourself and others more intimately, but also to guide and inspire your life.

The Healing Power of the Universe

Astrology shows us that the universe is holistic and interconnected. 'As above, so below' encapsulates the idea that what happens on earth corresponds to, reflects or is deeply connected with what happens in the heavens. Understanding this intimate connection offers you magical opportunities to harness the wisdom of the stars and tap into the healing power of the cosmos. The way in which the stars and planets aligned when you were born, and how they continue to align and form patterns as you move through your life, describes and impacts both your inner world and outer life circumstances.

The Astrology Fix brings the healing power of the universe right down to earth. It is a modern guide to the ancient practice of looking to the stars for inspiration, meaning and guidance, and offers a unique introduction to how you can use astrological wisdom in your daily life to maximize your chances of success, in the here and now and in the future. Designed for beginners and experts alike, the book contains quick and easy-to-implement fixes as well as opportunities for healing and growth for everyone, providing all the information and tools you need to become your own astrologer.

For most of us, our understanding of astrology begins and ends with our sun sign, or the sign we are born under. Your sun sign describes your identity and how your innate personality evolves through life. But as essential as your sun sign is to understanding and interpreting your astrological blueprint, it is just one component of your rich astrological personality, and the entry point to a wealth of astrological revelations. You are so much more than your sun sign. You are influenced by the sun, the moon, the planets and all the stars above. For example, your moon sign represents your inner emotional life, and your rising sign represents how others see you or the image you present to the world. The position of each of the other planets at the time of your birth represents a specific aspect or drive in your life. Together, all these elements blend to create an astrological outline of you, the natural gifts you were born with, and the combined power of the cosmic influences guiding all areas of your life.

How to Use This Book

The Astrology Fix will show you how to harness the power of your planets and learn to use the practical wisdom of astrology in your daily life. This can reveal a deeper understanding of yourself and others, as well as offer insights into how to deal with life's many challenges.

Chapter One explains what astrology is and why you need it. Your birth chart is a blueprint for your personality and you can use its wisdom to change your life for the better.

Chapters Two and Three introduce you to the power of your sun sign, and show how your birth chart relates to the whole universe. Calculate your rising and moon signs to reflect on your character and find out what motivates you. Discover the significance of the planets and how each body expresses itself according to the zodiac sign or house it occupies and the area of your life each house represents.

The driving force of the book is Chapter Four, which presents more than 50 unique cosmic practices and rituals, organized by key areas of your life, such as love and relationships and health and well-being, to help you create a holistic life plan. You can also turn to the 'Index by Need' (see page 174) to identify common emotional needs or life situations that you can draw down the healing power of the stars to help with. Whether you are dealing with a broken heart or a career setback, you will be directed to an appropriate astrological fix for your issue.

Note: This book primarily offers recommendations tailored to your sun, moon and rising signs, and there are charts to help you calculate these signs. When references are made to planets, it is recommended, but not essential, that you create a free birth chart.

THE SOUL MAP

Astrologers see the birth chart as a map for the soul.
Learn how to interpret yours to improve self-awareness
and nurture growth.

Astrology Today

Astrology is an ancient art. The first astrological birth charts are believed to have originated in ancient Egypt around 4500 BCE. The Babylonians created an astrology system around 1800 BCE, then, after the fall of Rome around 500 CE, the Greeks and Chinese developed their own systems. Although astrology then waned in popularity and influence, it never disappeared completely. However, it was not until the early twentieth century that interest in astrology re-emerged – not as a predictive or divinatory technique, but as a psychological tool for greater self-awareness.

The genesis of the New Age and self-help movements from the 1960s onwards significantly increased the popularity of astrology as a self-help tool. Modern Western astrology is now firmly rooted in the psychological and personal growth approach, with growing numbers of people seeking out a spiritual perspective. The art of astrology is no longer seen as something highly complicated which only professionally qualified astrologers can use; it is accepted as a popular and practical craft that anyone can learn about and apply to their daily life with positive and healing benefits.

Indeed, the millennial mystic renaissance suggests that astrology today goes way beyond newspaper-style sun-sign horoscopes. It can offer you the tools to understand yourself better and identify paths that can help you navigate life's opportunities and setbacks, heal your wounds and develop your full potential. And during times of stress, people find as much reassurance, hope and insight in astrology today as they did centuries ago.

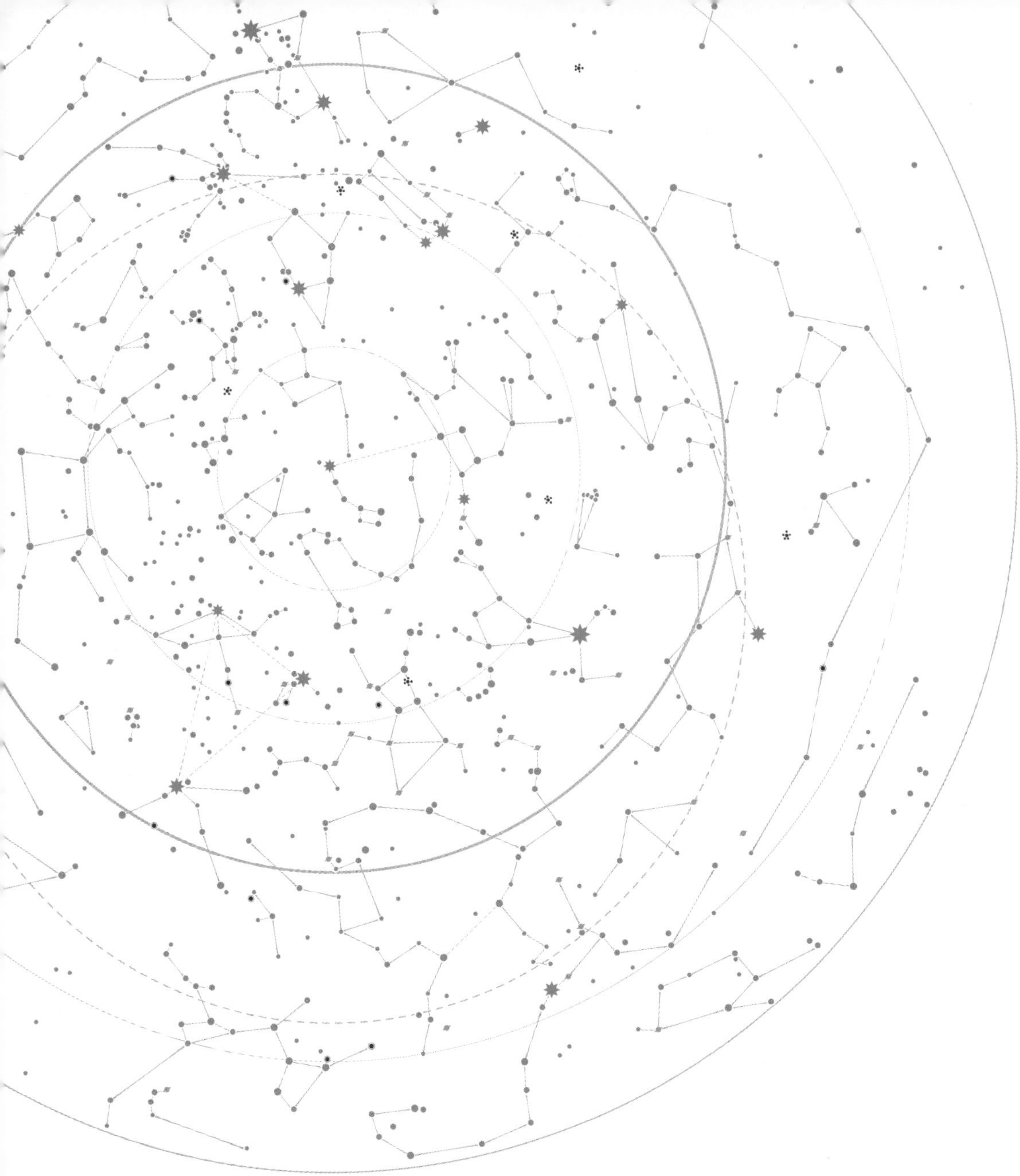

Your Astrological Blueprint

Your birth chart, or natal chart, is your astrological blueprint. It is a guide to the potential of your personality and your likely journey or evolution through life, according to the position of the planets in the sky at the time you were born.

Your birth chart can reveal your potential strengths as well as your possible weaknesses, or the challenges you need to overcome and learn from to evolve on your journey through life. It can also divulge the optimum time for you to make important decisions in your life and your compatibility with other people. You don't need to have your birth chart drawn up by a professional to get the most out of this book, but if you would like to have this done at some point, be aware that you will need to know the time, date and place of your birth.

If you're not sure what time you were born, ask your relatives first or do some research, but if nothing comes up, simply enter 12 noon. This does mean you can't accurately estimate your rising sign and other aspects of your birth chart, but don't despair as there is still much of value you can discover simply from your date of birth. Indeed, your birthday isn't just your special day, it is also the golden key to your astrological personality and deepest desires.

If you do decide to get your birth chart drawn up, it can reveal incredible insights about yourself and the areas of your life you are likely to flourish in. But be aware that what it reveals is *potential* only. Whether you develop that potential is up to you. You can choose to dance or you can choose to sleep under your stars.

Decoding Your Birth Chart

Your birth chart resembles a wheel. Decoding it can help you determine the position of the sun and the planets when you were born, which in turn will enable you to understand yourself and your life better. Be aware that the sun is the most powerful celestial and astrological body in your chart. Every month, and over the course of a year, it moves full circle through 12 astrological constellations or signs known as the zodiac: Aries, Taurus, Gemini, Cancer, Leo, Virgo, Libra, Scorpio, Sagittarius, Capricorn, Aquarius and Pisces. Each sign is also linked to one specific element – earth, air, fire or water – and its associated characteristics (see pages 26–27).

Here are some important terms you will need to know:

- **SUN SIGN**: the position of the sun and the zodiac sign it was passing through when you were born, and the most important part of your birth chart.
- **RISING SIGN**: the zodiac sign that was rising up when you were born. It is also known as the ascendant. Along with the moon sign, this is the next most important part of your birth chart.
- **MOON SIGN**: the position of the moon and the zodiac sign it was passing through when you were born.
- **THE PLANETS**: each planet was in a sign when you were born and will also impact your personality and potential (see page 66).
- **THE 12 HOUSES**: the first house on your birth chart is where your rising sign is located. From there, move anti-clockwise to discover which signs fall into the other 11 houses. Each house is associated with a different aspect of your personality and life (see page 69).

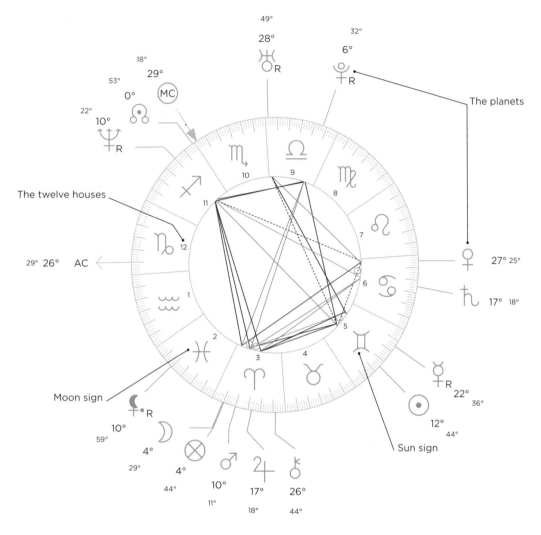

The planets

The twelve houses

29° 26° AC

Moon sign

Sun sign

PLANET SYMBOLS

| Sun: ☉ | Moon: ☽ | Mercury: ☿ | Venus: ♀ | Mars: ♂ | North Node: ☊ |
| Saturn: ♄ | Uranus: ♅ | Neptune: ♆ | Pluto: ♇ | Jupiter: ♃ | Part of Fortune: ⊗ |

ZODIAC SIGNS

| Aries: ♈ | Taurus: ♉ | Gemini: ♊ | Cancer: ♋ | Leo: ♌ | Virgo: ♍ |
| Libra: ♎ | Scorpio: ♏ | Sagittarius: ♐ | Capricorn: ♑ | Aquarius: ♒ | Pisces: ♓ |

Refining and Recording Your Birth Chart

To understand and interpret your birth chart, and become your own astrologer in the process, follow this step-by-step guide.

1 **Know your sun sign.** Who you are, your sense of self and what drives you are revealed by your sun sign. See page 24 to learn the meaning of your sun sign.

2 **Know your rising sign.** How other people see you or the image you present to the world can be found in your rising sign. See page 54 to identify your rising sign.

3 **Know your moon sign.** Your emotional self and inner world are defined by your moon sign. See page 60 to discover your moon sign.

4 **Know your planets.** Your personality traits, deepest desires and opportunities for growth are written in the stars. See page 66.

5 **Know your houses.** Different aspects of your life are represented by the different houses. See page 69.

6 **Know yourself.** At this stage, you may want to buy a blank notebook or diary to record any new insights from an astrological perspective. There's no predicting what treasures you might uncover about yourself and others in your life.

7 **Know peace.** Work through all the astrology fixes from page 70 onwards or choose the ones that seem most fitting to bring the cosmic forces in your life into balance, and heal, uplift and transform all areas of your life.

CHAPTER TWO

THE SUN SIGNS

Discover more about your astrological character and those around you. Use your discoveries to build on strengths, work with flaws and improve communication.

Your Sun Sign

This star is the most powerful force in your birth chart. It represents your creativity, your individuality and your character traits. It also represents the forces that drive you. Think of your sun sign as your ego, your essence and how you understand yourself. It is what is innate within you, and also your potential for personal growth and evolution. Understanding both the strengths and weaknesses of your sun sign can help you make better choices in life, but remember that you are much more than just your sun sign. Your moon and rising sign are also influential, as are other planets.

On the cusp

The dates when one sun sign changes to another can vary between the 18th and the 23rd of each month. If your birthday falls between those dates, you were born on the cusp of two signs. If this is the case, the sun sign that your birth date falls into will be your official sun sign, but you should also familiarize yourself with the qualities of the other sign. For example, if you were born on 21 September you are technically a perfectionist Virgo but may sometimes feel more like a balanced Libra.

Be aware that the zodiac mirrors the journey from birth to old age. It begins with Aries, who often showcase the innocence of a newborn, and each sign after Aries grows until the zodiac completes with Pisces, often thought of as the 'old soul'. This doesn't mean that all Arians are immature and all Pisceans are wise, just that each sun sign can teach us something important about different ages and stages of our lives.

Born under the 13th sign?

According to recent NASA reports there may be 13 rather than 12 star signs. The 13th sign is called Ophiuchus and would be the sun sign for anyone born between November 29 and December 17. However, astronomy is not astrology. Astrologers have known about the Ophiuchus constellation for thousands of years but choose to leave Ophiuchus out of the equation and correspond the Zodiac with the 12 months of the year. Perhaps this is because Ophiuchus shares many of the characteristics typically associated with Sagittarius, such as being a light bearer, healer and dreamer.

The Elements

Most of us know our sun sign, but do you know which element your sun sign is associated with?

The twelve signs of the zodiac are governed by the four elements – fire, earth, air and water – and each element has distinct qualities that influence its associated signs.

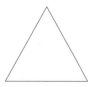

ARIES, **LEO** and **SAGITTARIUS** are governed by the element of fire. Passion, spontaneity and motivation are key words here. Like the element of fire itself, fire signs provide warmth and enlightenment, but they also have the potential to burn out quickly or to cause great destruction if their sizzling enthusiasm is not well managed.

CANCER, **SCORPIO** and **PISCES** are governed by the element of water. Intuitive, intense and emotional, water signs are often mysterious and illuminating. They have the ability to adapt themselves to every situation with skill and grace, but their emotional intensity can turn to possessiveness and paranoia if not kept in balance.

TAURUS, **VIRGO** and **CAPRICORN** are guided by the element of earth. Tactile, grounded and practical, they are the most down-to-earth signs of the zodiac. They are reliable and highly productive, providing firm foundations on which to build towards success, but they also have a tendency to focus too much on the material or superficial and neglect what truly matters.

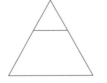

The element of air is the underlying force directing **GEMINI**, **LIBRA** and **AQUARIUS**. Communication, movement, adventure and inspiration are key words. Like a breath of fresh air, they can bring tremendous energy, insight and vision, but they can also be extremely unpredictable, depending on which direction the wind blows.

TRY THIS Arians need to learn the importance of patience and dedication to see things through and succeed. Practise the Aries Ritual for Motivation on page 75.

Aries: The Ram

21 March–19 April

You are a pioneer and one of life's movers and shakers. Daring and full of initiative, you push the boundaries. Your love of adventure and independent spirit makes you a natural leader and motivator.

SHINING QUALITIES

Enterprising
Courageous
Enthusiastic

SHADOW QUALITIES

Impatient
Ruthless
Tactless

RULING PLANET

Mars

AFFIRMATION

I can lead with gentleness.

WORK

Aries are drawn to roles where they can lead, motivate and inspire, and they tend to do well because they are driven and inspire passion in others. If Arians can't lead, they prefer to work alone and are great self-starters. They are skilled at initiating projects and need jobs that give them plenty of challenge and freedom of expression.

HOME

Aries are not natural home-makers. Their preference is to be out *doing*, and when at home they tend to work on projects to advance their career. However, they often require a place to retire to when they need to regroup, so they ensure that their home is exactly the way they want it to be.

PLEASURE

This is the sign that loves to move and be constantly on the go. Arians prefer to run rather than walk, and seek adventure and fun in all that they do.

ARIES IN SHADE

Their love of action means Arians suffer from a tendency to burn out quickly. They can be too impatient to finish tasks and quickly bore of routine. They can also be selfish, tactless and poor listeners, with their competitive nature making them especially bad losers.

TRY THIS Taureans tend to hold on to grudges and past wounds, which can keep them stuck in the past. Practise letting go with the Pisces Forgiveness Spell on page 99.

Taurus: The Bull

20 April–20 May

Born under the sign of the bull, you know what you want and are very good at getting it. Grounded and strong-willed, you are invaluable in a crisis. Your driving force is determination. A delightful combination of strength and softness, stability and creativity, you are blessed with natural charm.

SHINING QUALITIES
Resilient
Sensual
Tenacious

SHADOW QUALITIES
Stubborn
Inflexible
Risk-averse

RULING PLANET
Venus

AFFIRMATION
I can let go of what is holding me back.

WORK
Taureans are drawn to financially rewarding jobs. They tend to do well because they're ambitious and have a high level of endurance – pulling an all-nighter is par for the course. Taureans crave structure and they are experts in turning an idea into reality.

HOME
Quality means everything to the Taurean – they would rather do without than make do. Their home and everything in it matters. When a Taurean is on top form, their home is beautiful, with everything in its perfect place.

PLEASURE
This is the sign that most appreciates giving or receiving a good massage, sweating it out in a sauna or indulging in great food and drink.

TAURUS IN SHADE
Their love of routine means they can get stuck in a rut. They are also averse to change. Even if something is not working out, a Taurean is reluctant to shake things up. And they can be stubborn: Taureans like to work at their own pace and don't take kindly to being told what to do.

TRY THIS Geminis must learn to connect to deeper feelings and love themselves rather than looking for affirmation from others. Practise the Venus Self-Love Spell on page 92.

Gemini: The Twins

21 May–21 June

Born under the sign of the twins, you are blessed with great versatility. You thrive at multi-tasking and are a born communicator with considerable charm. Your driving force is curiosity. You love to learn and need to keep your agile mind constantly stimulated.

SHINING QUALITIES
Entertaining
Agile
Stimulating

SHADOW QUALITIES
Deceitful
Shallow
Poorly informed

RULING PLANET
Mercury

AFFIRMATION
I am a person of integrity and depth.

WORK
Geminis tend to be drawn to careers in the media, writing, advertising, politics, sales, teaching, or any career that requires great communication skills. Highly sociable, they work best when part of a team and in careers that offer plenty of variety.

HOME
Geminis rarely settle in one place for long. They love to experience new locations but, wherever they go, they ensure that their homes are welcoming and warm places in which to entertain.

PLEASURE
Mental and physical challenge is important. Their constant need to stretch themselves gives them an infectious, youthful energy. Routine is something they don't cope well with.

GEMINI IN SHADE
A love of constant stimulation means that Geminis risk becoming depressed when confined by routine. They can be superficial and unwilling to look beneath the surface of things or within themselves for answers. They can also be trouble-making gossips.

TRY THIS Cancerians are sometimes overly anxious and defensive, which can lead to misunderstandings and feelings of isolation. Practise the Clarity of Mind Visualization on page 118.

Cancer: The Crab

22 June–22 July

Your driving force is intuition. A fascinating combination of mystery and openness, gentleness and resilience, you are sensitive and giving and you inspire others to be emotionally honest.

SHINING QUALITIES
Compassionate
Imaginative
Gentle

SHADOW QUALITIES
Protective
Defensive
Moody

RULING PLANET
The moon

AFFIRMATION
I can love and trust myself completely.

WORK
Cancerians do well in careers that utilize their powerful intuition. They are often drawn to jobs that involve mentoring, caring for, nurturing or helping others. They may also gravitate towards careers that are artistic and creative in some way.

HOME
Home is where the heart of a Cancer-born person is likely to be. Their home is their cosy sanctuary, a place where they can withdraw to and shut out the world.

PLEASURE
Helping others gives this sign tremendous pleasure. They love to nurture, protect, advise and care for others and they make truly loyal and wonderful friends.

CANCER IN SHADE
Their love of helping others can mean they forget to tend to their own needs. There is a tendency to worry, be overprotective and controlling. If things don't go their way, Cancerians retreat into their shell. They can also hold very deep grudges and be emotionally manipulative.

TRY THIS Leos tend to hog the limelight and ignore the opinions of others, which can make them enemies. Practise the Cancer Ritual for Better Communication on page 96.

Leo: The Lion

23 July–22 August

Born under the sign of the lion, you tend to ooze charisma and self-confidence. You are warm-hearted and visionary – your driving force is your huge heart. Generous and bold, with a larger-than-life personality, you like to live your life to the full.

SHINING QUALITIES
Sunny-natured
Passionate
Glamorous

SHADOW QUALITIES
Arrogant
Narcissistic
Attention-seeking

RULING PLANET
The sun

AFFIRMATION
I can shine and encourage others to shine with me.

WORK
Leos bring laughter and light to any situation and are well suited to careers that use their creative and visionary abilities. They make great managers, bosses and entrepreneurs, sensing trends before others do and leading the way for others to follow.

HOME
Luxury means everything to Leos – they need to be surrounded by both beauty and comfort. Their home and everything in it will look expensive and tasteful, but it will also feel inviting and warm.

PLEASURE
This sign loves the good life and takes great pleasure in delicious food and wine and the company of others. Leos are typically the life and soul of the party.

LEO IN SHADE
Without rest, Leos need to always shine can lead to burnout. There is also a tendency towards arrogance and an unhealthy dependence on the admiration of others for validation. They can suffer from hurt pride very easily if others disagree with them, and they boast to mask their insecurities.

TRY THIS Virgos tend to minimize their own needs in favour of those of others. Practise the Sun-Sign Self-Care fix on page 114.

Virgo: The Virgin

23 August–22 September

Trustworthy and hardworking, with immaculate timing and presentation, your presence is often a healing one. You are organized, efficient, practical and showcase razor-sharp perception and insight. You are quietly creative and pay attention to detail. Your driving force is towards perfection.

SHINING QUALITIES
Insightful
Considerate
Refined

SHADOW QUALITIES
Pedantic
Critical of self and others
Fussy

RULING PLANET
Mercury

AFFIRMATION
I can focus on the power and magic of the now.

WORK
Virgos may be drawn to work that requires concentration and close attention to detail. Their quick, analytical mind, reliability and courteous manner make them essential-team players who are often the backbone of an organisation.

HOME
Virgos take great pride in an organized, clean and tidy home. Everything will have its place, and there will be a minimum of clutter but an abundance of beautiful detail.

PLEASURE
Virgos have a fastidious approach to life, and any unhealthy habits will be minimized. They have an incredible work ethic and any downtime will be scheduled and productive rather than restful.

VIRGO IN SHADE
With their passion for perfection, Virgos can be extremely hard on both themselves and others. They can set impossible standards and be super-critical and fussy. Their painstaking attention to detail also means they often lose sight of the bigger picture and the joy of what they are involved with.

TRY THIS Librans can be superficial at times and this will push authentic people away. Practise the Inner Power Visualization on page 94.

Libra: The Scales

23 September–22 October

Born under the sign of the scales, you are open-minded and passionately believe in justice. Your driving force is harmony. You have an amazing ability to find the perfect compromise and see every side of the argument. Idealistic and diplomatic, you dream of a more peaceful world.

SHINING QUALITIES

Fair

Peace-loving

Elegant

SHADOW QUALITIES

Indecisive

Needy

Lazy

RULING PLANET

Venus

AFFIRMATION

I can listen to my inner voice and follow the answers there.

WORK

Librans are often drawn to justice and the law, and any work that requires diplomacy and tact. Their love of beauty may also draw them to artistic endeavours but, whatever they do, they always bring harmony and balance to the work place.

HOME

Librans like their homes to be luxurious and beautiful, but even more important to them is comfort. They want their private space to be as relaxing, harmonious and peaceful as possible.

PLEASURE

With their taste for the good things in life, Librans love to eat the finest foods and to wear the finest clothes. They have exquisite taste and, whatever their budget, will look like a million dollars.

LIBRA IN SHADE

Indecisive to a fault, Librans can adjust their behaviour to suit others and become untrustworthy and less credible in the process. They can also be extremely self-indulgent, materialistic, shallow and vain. They hate being alone and can become dependent in relationships.

TRY THIS Scorpios find it almost impossible to admit they are wrong or to learn from their mistakes. Practise the Learning from Yourself fix on page 142.

Scorpio: The Scorpion

23 October–21 November

You are a dynamic achiever, capable of beating the odds. You have tremendous willpower and enviable determination. Deep and intense, you can see right to the heart of the matter. Your driving force is self-control.

SHINING QUALITIES
Resilient
Penetrating
Intuitive

SHADOW QUALITIES
Vindictive
Controlling
Jealous

RULING PLANETS
Mars and Pluto

AFFIRMATION
I can forgive myself and others.

WORK
Scorpions are drawn to leadership roles, but whatever work they do their gut instincts guide them. Great motivators, they have a remarkable ability to focus on what matters most and see beneath the superficial, which can make them a tremendous force for good in the world.

HOME
Scorpios love the idea of regeneration and their homes are often in a state of transformation as they experiment with different styles. Whatever theme they choose, they will demonstrate a taste for the dramatic or unusual.

PLEASURE
Scorpio is a deeply passionate sign and Scorpios often have a number of loyal friends and admirers. Taking it easy doesn't come naturally to people born under this sign; they love to work and play hard.

SCORPIO IN SHADE
Scorpios have a tendency towards self-destructive and addictive behaviour. In relationships their fear of being alone can make them jealous, manipulative and controlling. They can also bear grudges and be hypocritical, accusing others of what they themselves are guilty of.

TRY THIS Sagittarians are full of optimistic potential but turning their brilliant ideas into reality can be a struggle. Try the Sagittarius Focus Mantra on page 125.

Sagittarius: The Archer

22 November–21 December

Born under the sign of the archer, you are a seeker of knowledge and thrive on challenges. You are an optimist and risk-taker with an insatiable appetite for life. Your thinking is philosophical and you are imaginative and creative.

SHINING QUALITIES
Adventurous

Charming

Far-sighted

SHADOW QUALITIES
Scattered

Restless

Unreliable

RULING PLANET
Jupiter

AFFIRMATION
I can seek the extraordinary in the ordinary.

WORK
Sagittarians are drawn to careers that offer freedom, travel and stimulation. Whatever field they choose, the most important consideration is that it is challenging and provides an opportunity to learn new things.

HOME
The home of a Sagittarian will have a bohemian feel. They don't tend to value material things and hate being tied to one place, but when they find the home of their dreams, it becomes their haven.

PLEASURE
One of the most energetic signs, Sagittarians love to eat heartily and burn it off with vigorous exercise. Being physically or intellectually tested is what truly fulfils them.

SAGITTARIUS IN SHADE
Sagittarians can be wildly uninhibited at times and this can come across as rudeness. Their restless nature also means they are prone to carelessness and a scattered, unproductive approach to life. In relationships, commitment is an issue.

TRY THIS Capricorn ambition means many are workaholics in danger of experiencing emotional burnout and losing motivation. Try the Calm Down Ritual on page 150.

Capricorn: The Goat

22 December–19 January

Patient and persistent, disciplined and reliable, you have the willpower to succeed. Your driving force is ambition. Your practicality, wisdom and strong sense of justice make you a person of honour and integrity.

SHINING QUALITIES
Courageous
Dependable
Determined

SHADOW QUALITIES
Materialistic
Narrow-minded
Pessimistic

RULING PLANET
Saturn

AFFIRMATION
I can be both ambitious and caring.

WORK
Capricorns are drawn to careers in which there is a clear structure so that they can achieve something meaningful, and climb the ladder of success. They excel in work that offers them an opportunity to mentor and advise. Capricorns love nothing more than to be the person people turn to in times of crisis.

HOME
Those born under this sign value material possessions highly. They choose properties that are sound investments for their future and take the very best care of them.

PLEASURE
Capricorns need reminding of the importance of rest and relaxation in their lives. With their unbeatable work ethic, unwinding on a regular basis is essential for their well-being.

CAPRICORN IN SHADE
Ruthless and ambitious, Capricorns can hurt others to get to where they want to be. Their preoccupation with material things means they easily lose sight of what truly matters, while their cautiousness can lead to missed opportunities.

Aquarius: The Water-Carrier

20 January–18 February

You have a vision for a better world and the determination and discipline to create positive change. Your driving force is humanitarianism. Highly original and innovative, you are often way ahead of your time.

SHINING QUALITIES
Original
Visionary
Idealistic

SHADOW QUALITIES
Chaotic
Stubborn
Rebellious

RULING PLANETS
Saturn and Uranus

AFFIRMATION
I can express my originality with compassion.

WORK
Aquarians need a career that offers them an opportunity to be inventive, creative and original. They excel in anything that helps human beings learn and progress in some way.

HOME
The homes of people born under this sign may be quirky or have highly unusual features. Aquarians may prefer to build their own homes from scratch or modify existing properties in some original way.

PLEASURE
Aquarian downtime is likely spent engaging in some eccentric or unusual hobby or interest that they are passionate about, from sky-diving to science-fiction conventions.

AQUARIUS IN SHADE
Aquarians can be unpredictable and unnecessarily rebellious at times. They are prone to crankiness and cynicism, so others often feel they must walk on eggshells around them. They can be insensitive and tactless, and become so driven that loved ones are neglected.

TRY THIS Pisceans often lose sight of their own identity and needs due to putting others first. Practise the Colour Visualisation for Protection fix on page 167.

Pisces: The Fish

19 February–20 March

You are deeply sensitive to the needs of others and never miss an opportunity to do good, where you can. Generous to a fault, your driving force is compassion. Your powerful intuition and ability to see the bigger picture means that you can make your life as enchanting as your dreams.

SHINING QUALITIES
Imaginative
Artistic
Compassionate

SHADOW QUALITIES
Indecisive
Unrealistic
Co-dependent

RULING PLANETS
Jupiter and Neptune

AFFIRMATION
I can dream of success and beauty for myself.

WORK
Pisceans are multi-talented and can adapt to almost any situation. As long as they listen to their intuition, they have the determination and intelligence to succeed at whatever they focus on.

HOME
The Piscean home is almost always exquisitely beautiful. Being sensitive souls, they also want it to be a safe and peaceful haven that they can retreat to if they feel overwhelmed.

PLEASURE
Pisceans often prioritize the well-being of others over their own and derive great pleasure from caring for others. Downtime is crucial for Pisceans, because having sufficient dream-time is essential to them.

PISCES IN SHADE
Instead of tackling their own fears and issues, Pisceans can easily lose their sense of self by immersing themselves in someone else's life or adapting their personality to accommodate others. They are also prone to chronic indecision, endlessly weighing up pros and cons but doing nothing to move their lives forward.

CHAPTER THREE

THE UNIVERSE

Calculate the influence of the stars, planets, houses,
moon and your rising sign. Study their dynamic interplay
to deepen and refine your interpretations and expand
your potential.

Your Rising Sign

While your sun sign reflects your unconscious true self, or who you really are, the first impression that you give out – the person people see when they meet you – is defined by your rising sign. This is the ascendant, the sign that was rising on the eastern horizon on the day you were born and is your conscious or 'outer' self and the 'persona' you present to the world. It's how you first come across to others or how you want them to see you. You can compare it to the door of a house – the entry point others first encounter and need to move through before taking a look at the house itself.

How to Calculate Your Rising Sign

You need to know your sun sign and the time you were born to calculate your rising sign. Look down the left-hand column in the table opposite to find your star sign. Then move along until you come to the two-hour window in which you were born. Be aware that the chart opposite is based on GMT, so there may be time differences to take into account. To calculate your rising sign, find out what time you were born and convert the time into GMT then compare it to the chart. If you don't know the time you were born, use 12 noon as your reference, but be aware that this won't produce the same level of accuracy as knowing your exact time of birth.

Rising Sign Chart

YOUR HOUR OF BIRTH (GMT)

YOUR SUN SIGN	6am to 8am	8am to 10am	10am to 12pm	12pm to 2pm	2pm to 4pm	4pm to 6pm	6pm to 8pm	8pm to 10pm	10pm to 12am	12am to 2am	2am to 4am	4am to 6am
♈ Aries	♉	♊	♋	♌	♍	♎	♏	♐	♑	♒	♓	♈
♉ Taurus	♊	♋	♌	♍	♎	♏	♐	♑	♒	♓	♈	♉
♊ Gemini	♋	♌	♍	♎	♏	♐	♑	♒	♓	♈	♉	♊
♋ Cancer	♌	♍	♎	♏	♐	♑	♒	♓	♈	♉	♊	♋
♌ Leo	♍	♎	♏	♐	♑	♒	♓	♈	♉	♊	♋	♌
♍ Virgo	♎	♏	♐	♑	♒	♓	♈	♉	♊	♋	♌	♍
♎ Libra	♏	♐	♑	♒	♓	♈	♉	♊	♋	♌	♍	♎
♏ Scorpio	♐	♑	♒	♓	♈	♉	♊	♋	♌	♍	♎	♏
♐ Sagittarius	♑	♒	♓	♈	♉	♊	♋	♌	♍	♎	♏	♐
♑ Capricorn	♒	♓	♈	♉	♊	♋	♌	♍	♎	♏	♐	♑
♒ Aquarius	♓	♈	♉	♊	♋	♌	♍	♎	♏	♐	♑	♒
♓ Pisces	♈	♉	♊	♋	♌	♍	♎	♏	♐	♑	♒	♓

Rising Fire Sign

If **Aries, Leo** or **Sagittarius** is on the ascendant, your outer manner is likely to make you appear energetic, upbeat and positive. There is typically a warmth and charisma about you. People gravitate towards you and often find it easy to confide in you because of your friendly and engaging persona.

- **ARIES** rising presents a bold and brave presence. You are passionate and inspiring and like to live your life in the fast lane. You are original and not afraid to be brutally honest.
- **LEO** rising shows confidence and dignity. You are someone who stands out from the crowd and there may be a rock-star vibe about you. You love to be noticed and expect to be adored.
- **SAGITTARIUS** rising offers an optimistic and enthusiastic presence. There is an infectious, light-hearted, free-spirited energy about you. You are dynamic and enterprising, and someone people naturally turn to for advice.

Rising Water Sign

If **Cancer**, **Scorpio** or **Pisces** is on the ascendant, your outer manner is likely to make you appear sensitive and elusive, sometimes to the point of aloofness. Your approach is typically intelligent but also intense. With you, still waters very much run deep.

- **CANCER** rising presents a nurturing and wise presence. You sometimes come across as shy and defensive, but this is because you are feeling your way into things. You can also appear seductive and mesmerizing.
- **SCORPIO** rising shows a smouldering intensity. You are a mystery whom others often find hard to read, but your mystery is also the source of your charisma and why people feel so drawn to you.
- **PISCES** rising offers a soft, vulnerable and gentle persona, but one that is also insightful, mystical and wise. Compassionate and with a spiritually healing presence that calms others, you frequently have a bewitching quality about you.

Rising Earth Sign

If **Taurus, Virgo** or **Capricorn** is on the ascendant, your outer manner is likely to make you appear organized, neat and grounded. There is typically a serious and earnest air about you. People sense that you are a dependable person and feel reassured by your reliability and inner calm.

- **TAURUS** rising presents a sensual but focused presence. You show others how to work hard and live the good life at the same time. You are down to earth and loyal.
- **VIRGO** rising shows intelligence and capability. You are meticulous and have an efficient and refined or tidy persona. You are someone who works very hard to improve not just your own life but the lives of others.
- **CAPRICORN** rising offers a diplomatic, reserved but pleasant presence. You are responsible, follow the rules and have a very realistic approach to life. You are as solid as a rock and can be depended on.

Rising Air Sign

If **Gemini, Libra** or **Aquarius** is on the ascendant, your outer manner is likely to make you appear highly sociable. Although communicative and easy to approach, you are also an independent spirit. Sometimes aloof, you are never short of ideas or the right words to express them eloquently.

- **GEMINI** rising presents a talkative and busy persona. You love to communicate with everyone about everything. You are fast moving with your words and, when you are around, life is never dull.
- **LIBRA** rising shows a tranquil and beautiful image to the world. You are calm and considered and can see all sides of an argument. You have a remarkable ability to make everyone feel special and valued.
- **AQUARIUS** rising offers a visionary and free-spirited presence. You appear intelligent and informed and there is often a slightly eccentric or off-the-wall air about you. A real trendsetter, you inspire hope for a better world.

Your Moon Sign

While your rising sign is your outer presence, the moon sign is your inner presence. It represents you from the inside out. It is your unconscious instincts and inner emotional life. In essence, it is the part of you that you keep hidden from the world; the part of you that only you can really know well. Your moon sign is where your emotions and deepest dreams and desires reside. Understanding the influences of your moon sign can not only lead to greater self-awareness and personal fulfilment, but also increase your chances of finding lasting love and fulfilling relationships.

How to Calculate Your Moon Sign

To determine your moon sign you need to have your birth chart drawn up or use special tables. Perhaps the simplest way to find out your moon sign is to use one of the free online calculators (see page 175). You just need to type in your birth date, the AM or PM time you were born and the time zone you were born in.

Moon in Fire Sign

If your moon sign is in **Aries, Leo** or **Sagittarius,** your inner child will typically be bursting with energy and passion. You approach life in a trusting, open-hearted and excitable way.

- Moon in **ARIES** people are bravehearts. You feel your way through life in a playful and adventurous way. You need to take the initiative and are daring and spontaneous with your heart. You truly believe in love at first sight and your greatest fear is a life without love.
- Moon in **LEO** people have a need to be admired and adored. An incurable romantic, you are generous and larger than life with your feelings, and loyalty matters greatly to you in a relationship. Your greatest fear is being ignored.
- Moon in **SAGITTARIUS** people love their freedom. Your heart doesn't take kindly to anything or anyone who can limit your liberty. You thrive whenever there is change, and your greatest fear is to get stuck in a rut.

Moon in Water Sign

If your moon sign is in **Cancer, Scorpio** or **Pisces**, your inner child needs to be creative and allowed to dream. You feel things very deeply and take everyone and everything in your life to heart.

- Moon in **CANCER** people only feel secure when they are loved. You truly feel your way through life and tend to be highly intuitive. You are sensitive to atmospheres and the feelings of others. You love to care for others. Your greatest fear is being alone.
- Moon in **SCORPIO** people are drawn to what is invisible and unseen. You approach life with great passion and intensity. Mysterious, you need to feel in control of your heart. Your greatest fear is rejection.
- Moon in **PISCES** people are warm and tender-hearted. You fine-tune your actions to the needs of others. Romantic and artistic, you were born to fall in love, but do need regular time alone to dream and recharge. Your greatest fear is loneliness.

Moon in Earth Sign

If your moon sign is in **Taurus, Virgo** or **Capricorn,** your inner child craves comfort and security, both emotionally and materially. You approach life in a cautious, practical and down-to-earth way.

- Moon in **TAURUS** people are calm and measured. You feel your way through life in a balanced and stable way. You crave stability in your relationships and understand that they need careful nurturing. Your greatest fear is that your trust and love will be betrayed.
- Moon in **VIRGO** people protect their hearts very carefully. You approach life in a detailed and cautious way and show your love by doing things for others rather than displays of emotion. Your greatest fear is being vulnerable.
- Moon in **CAPRICORN** people like to feel they are responsible. You see life through the lens of logic and reason, and are not prone to emotional outbursts or spontaneity. Your greatest fear is losing control of your emotions.

Moon in Air Sign

If your moon sign is in **Gemini, Libra** or **Aquarius**, your inner child requires constant stimulation and entertainment. You love to be surprised and approach life in an inquisitive and restless way.

- Moon in **GEMINI** people adore conversation and networking. You approach life with childlike curiosity, but prefer to endlessly flirt with rather than commit to new possibilities. Your greatest fear is boredom.
- Moon in **LIBRA** people love to share, and do almost anything to keep the peace. You feel your way through life in a harmony-loving way. You are searching for your soul mate or other half. Your greatest fear is not being able to find a compromise.
- Moon in **AQUARIUS** people try to apply reason to every situation. You are altruistic, always thinking of what will help others or serve the greater good. Your greatest fear is that your life did not make a difference.

The Planets

Your sun, rising and moon signs are the most powerful influences in your life, but the position of the planets in your birth chart also play a part. They represent basic drives or psychological traits within your personality. To determine where the planets are in your birth chart, you will need to have it drawn up. However, it can be helpful to know about the influences of all the planets, and in Chapter Four, you will be shown ways to harness those influences, regardless of which planet rules your sun sign.

The planets are divided into three categories: personal, social and collective.

The **sun, moon, Mercury, Venus** and **Mars** are considered to be personal planets because they represent core personality traits.

Jupiter and Saturn are social planets as they represent our connection to family and other people.

Uranus, Neptune and **Pluto** are collective planets in that they represent collective social and cultural ideas.

Chiron is a planet that belongs in all three categories because it unites personal, social and collective themes.

- **THE SUN**: your core being
- **THE MOON**: your instincts
- **MERCURY**: how you think and communicate
- **VENUS**: your relationships
- **MARS**: where you direct your energy
- **JUPITER**: the realm of ideas and travel
- **SATURN**: the need for discipline and structure
- **URANUS**: enlightenment and change
- **NEPTUNE**: inspiration and idealism
- **PLUTO:** power and transformation
- **CHIRON:** healing and evolution

The Houses

The 12 houses in a birth chart relate to different areas of your life. If you have your birth chart drawn up, you can find out which planet or planets are in each house and how those planets influence that particular area of experience. Your rising sign is always going to be located in the first house on your birth chart. The first house occupies the nine o'clock position on your chart, is ruled by Aries and represents your self-image and appearance. From the first house, the other houses circle backwards around the wheel of your birth chart, in an anti-clockwise direction.

FIRST HOUSE

Self-image and appearance – Aries

SECOND HOUSE

Values and income – Taurus

TWELFTH HOUSE

Karma and healing – Pisces

THIRD HOUSE

Mind and communication – Gemini

ELEVENTH HOUSE

Friendships and community – Aquarius

FOURTH HOUSE

Home and family – Cancer

TENTH HOUSE

Career and destiny – Capricorn

FIFTH HOUSE

Creativity and individuality – Leo

NINTH HOUSE

Learning and travel – Sagittarius

SIXTH HOUSE

Routine and health – Virgo

EIGHTH HOUSE

Sex and transformation – Scorpio

SEVENTH HOUSE

Love and relationships – Libra

Getting Your Astrology Fix

Whether you decide to get your birth chart drawn up or not, you can get your astrology fix for every area of your life simply by knowing your sun sign and by working through the rituals, meditations and strategies in the next chapter.

CHAPTER FOUR

YOUR
ASTROLOGY FIX

Bring cosmic forces into balance with over 50 powerful
astrological fixes designed to transform your
emotional, physical and spiritual life,
today and every day of your future.

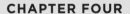

JOY AND SUCCESS

The astrology fixes in this section are designed to help you harness the power of the stars to attract abundance, optimism, luck, empowerment, joy and success into all areas of your life.

> **TRY THIS** Focus your energy on what you want to manifest. Harnessing the energy of Mars by writing down your goals can give you a potent motivational boost.

Aries Ritual for Motivation

Aries kick-starts the astrological year with tremendous enthusiasm and drive, but this can wane as the year progresses. If you have Aries as your sun sign or Aries rising, this ritual can turbocharge your momentum. If Aries is not your sun or rising sign, use this ritual for empowerment by tuning into the motivational energy of the planet Mars, which rules Aries.

YOU WILL NEED
- A pen
- A notepad
- Your intention

STEPS
1. Place a pen and notepad beside your bed.
2. Before you go to bed, read about the sun sign Aries on page 28 and the planet Mars on page 66.
3. Grab your pen and notepad and draw the symbol for Aries. Then draw the symbol for the planet Mars alongside it.
4. Beneath those two symbols write down your goals for the following day.
5. Close your eyes and visualize the two symbols you drew.
6. Then, imagine yourself completing those goals with Arian energy motivating and empowering you and increasing your chances of success.

Jupiter Mantra for a Brighter Future

If you have Sagittarius as your sun or rising sign, repeating this mantra can be a positive reminder of your natural instinct to look on the bright side. If Sagittarius is not your sun or rising sign, use this mantra to harness the power of Jupiter – the planet of faith, joy and positivity that rules Sagittarius.

YOU WILL NEED

- The day to be a Thursday
- A picture of the planet Jupiter

STEPS

1 Every Thursday – the day of the week ruled by the planet Jupiter (see page 135) – set aside a few minutes to sit somewhere quiet where you won't be disturbed.
2 Close your eyes and take a few deep breaths until you feel relaxed.
3 Visualize the image of Jupiter.
4 Repeat this mantra out loud, slowly and steadily, 10 times: 'Jupiter, bring me my joy.' As you speak, concentrate on the sound of the words. Coordinate your speech with your breath so you say the first three words on an inhale and the second part on an exhale.
5 Repeat the mantra silently, with just your lips moving.
6 Then, repeat the mantra in your thoughts.
7 Visualize the picture of Jupiter again and, before you open your eyes, smile broadly.

TRY THIS This spell is especially beneficial when performed on a Saturday as this is the day associated with the disciplined and hard-working planet Saturn, which rules Capricorn.

Capricorn Visualization for Wealth

If you have Capricorn as your sun or rising sign, this visualization can help attract wealth to you and remind you of your own inner glow. If Capricorn is not your sun or rising sign, use this spell to harness the discipline, willpower and intense focus of this earth sign to draw wealth and prosperity into your life.

YOU WILL NEED
- A long white candle
- An open heart and mind

STEPS
1 Light the white candle and place it safely and securely in front of you.
2 Study the Capricorn sun sign symbol on page 44 of this book.
3 Stare gently into the glow surrounding the candle flame for a few moments, making sure not to look directly into the flame.
4 Feel the candle's heat. Let it remind you of the warmth within your heart.
5 Close your eyes and concentrate on the dark imprint left there from watching the flame.
6 Visualize the Capricorn symbol again, then imagine the type of wealth you wish to manifest in your life. For example, if you want to attract money, visualize your bank account growing. If you desire happiness, imagine yourself going about your life with a genuine smile on your face.
7 Keep your eyes closed and continue to visualize until the imprint left by the flame has vanished.
8 Safely extinguish the flame and carry that feeling of abundance within you.

> **TRY THIS** Before finding success, comedian Jim Carrey wrote himself a cheque for $10million dated 10 years in the future. He was later paid this for a movie. Carry your cheque with you and take it out whenever you need reminding of your contract with the law of abundance.

Scorpio Contract for Abundance

People with Scorpio sun or rising signs are born with leadership potential that is a success magnet. This exercise is a sacred contract between Scorpios and the universe to attract abundance, and is a first step towards wish fulfilment. Non-Scorpios should perform this ritual to align with the energy and drive of this water sign and create the mindset to invite abundance into their lives.

YOU WILL NEED

- A piece of white paper or card
- A ruler
- A pen (ideally a fountain pen)

STEPS

1 On the piece of paper or card, use the ruler and pen to draw a pretend cheque and make it out to yourself.
2 Write down a future date in the date section of the cheque.
3 In the amount section, fill in the amount of money or form of abundance you desire. Keep it realisitic.
4 In the 'paid by' section write 'the law of abundance.'
5 Sign the cheque and visualize yourself already having the funds.

Full Moon Luck and Empowerment Chant

This chant is designed to attract luck and give you a boost of confidence, and must be performed when the moon is full. It is perfect for those born with Cancer as their sun or rising sign, given that the moon rules Cancer, but is empowering for every sun sign because the intuitive and luck-enhancing energies associated with lunar power are at their height when the moon is full.

YOU WILL NEED

- A view of the full moon (see page 175 for moon calendar resource)

STEPS

1 Find a place – indoors or outdoors – where you can see the full moon.
2 Look at the moon and visualize moonlight flowing into you.
3 Raise your hands in front of you with your palms facing upwards.
4 Imagine yourself catching the moonlight and feeling its power.
5 Visualize moonlight washing all over you.
6 When you feel bathed in moonlight, chant the following out loud: 'Dear moon, bless me with your light and luck. Let me shine forever bright.'
7 Thank the moon and return to your evening.

TRY THIS Practise the Finding Harmony Exercise on page 151 to help you find balance with opposite zodiac powers.

Libra Harmony Meditation

Organization is key to prioritizing your goals and finding focus in both work and life, and the sun sign to teach us this life-enhancing power is Libra. This morning ritual will resonate powerfully with people who have Libra as their sun or rising sign, but will also help other sun signs create order and harmony in their lives.

YOU WILL NEED

- An alarm

STEPS

1   Before you go to sleep, set your alarm to wake you up 10 minutes earlier than normal.
2   Once you are in bed, refer to the Libran symbol of the balanced scales on page 55. Keep this image of harmony in your mind as you settle and go to sleep.
3   The next morning, when your alarm goes off, let your first thoughts be of the balanced scales.
4   Use the 10 minutes to do some gentle stretching, then sit quietly and reflect calmly on your day ahead and what you hope to achieve.

> **TRY THIS** If you practice yoga and are familiar with this pose, you may also want to attempt the full sun salute pose.

Salute to the Sun Stretch

Perform this sun salute to invite the sun's warmth, laughter and inspiration into your life. Those born with Leo as their sun or rising sign will have a natural affinity with this exercise, but it can be performed by every sun sign to help them tap into their inner confidence and joy, and increase their energy.

YOU WILL NEED

- Space
- Your intention
- A sunny day

STEPS

1 Stand with feet hip-width apart, arms by your sides. Breathe deeply and slowly.
2 Place your hands in front of your chest, palms together, in the prayer position.
3 Set your intention, which is to feel joy.
4 Raise your prayer hands towards the ceiling in a salute, and gently arch your back as you look up at your hands.
5 As you stretch, keep your chest open and visualize a lion, the symbol of Leo, basking in the sun.
6 Inhale deeply and feel yourself drinking in the energy and warmth of the sun.
7 Exhale and drop your arms back to your sides.

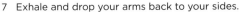

TRY THIS Instead of using just one candle, you may want to light a candle in each colour simultaneously to enhance the positive energies of this wishing incantation.

Gemini Laughter Incantation

The ideal time to speak this incantation is between 21 May and 21 June, when the sun is in the mercurial and expressive sign of Gemini. But you can also perform it at any time of the year to give yourself a much-needed happiness boost. People with Gemini as their sun or rising sign will find this incantation particularly useful, but every sun sign will benefit from the magic of laughter.

YOU WILL NEED
- A trusting and open heart
- A yellow, white or red candle

STEPS
1 Light your yellow (for positivity), white (for intention) or red (for courage) candle and place it securely in front of you.
2 Close your eyes and place one hand on your heart and the other on your forehead.
3 Visualize the symbol for the sun sign Gemini (see page 55), and consider its potential for self-expression, connection and happiness.
4 Speak this incantation: 'Laughter and joy come into my life. I open my mind and my heart to both of you. I am happy. I am free.'
5 Repeat the incantation and, this time, laugh as you say it.
6 Open your eyes, blow out the candle, and feel yourself connecting to your inner light.

TRY THIS Certain gemstones have long been considered lucky for their specific sun signs (shown opposite). Do bear these in mind, but the aim is to find the good luck birthstone that speaks most to you.

Zodiac Good-Luck Charm

Good-luck charms really can work: psychologists believe the personal associations you have with a specific charm can activate centres in your brain that boost confidence or make you feel lucky. And when you feel lucky you are more likely to attract success. The key words here are 'personal associations', and one highly effective way to personalize a good-luck charm is to choose one based on the characteristics of your sun sign.

YOU WILL NEED
- Your own good-luck charm

STEPS

1 Read up about your sun sign (see pages 28–51).

2 Choose a good-luck gemstone charm based on the characteristics of your sun sign. You may want to refer to the recommendations opposite or you can choose one yourself. Just make sure, in your own mind, that it connects to the energies of your sun sign.

3 Carry your zodiac good-luck charm everywhere, trusting that it will help you to feel lucky.

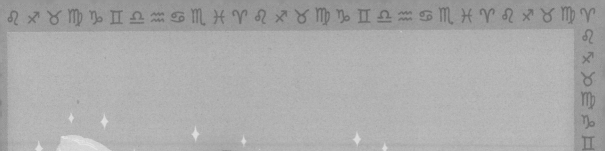

ARIES
Diamond

TAURUS
Emerald

GEMINI
Pearl

CANCER
Ruby

LEO
Peridot

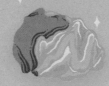

LIBRA
Opal

VIRGO
Sapphire

SCORPIO
Topaz

SAGITTARIUS
Turquoise

CAPRICORN
Garnet

AQUARIUS
Amethyst

PISCES
Aquamarine

LOVE AND RELATIONSHIPS

You can call on the energy of the stars to promote self-love, forgiveness, trust and communication, all of which can improve your relationships.

> **TRY THIS** Don't forget to give yourself permission to laugh, feel emotional or awkward. It might be embarrassing to see yourself in a reflection talking to yourself. Shake this off through daily practise to shine brightly.

Permission to Shine Chant

If we're entirely honest, it's sometimes hard to like let alone love ourselves. Use this liking-yourself chant to align with the shining potential of your sun sign and boost your self-esteem whenever you feel unhappy with yourself.

YOU WILL NEED
- A handheld or vanity mirror

STEPS
1. Hold up the mirror to your face to see yourself intimately.
2. Meet your reflection as an old friend and hold your gaze.
3. Study how beautiful your eyes are.
4. Repeat the following chant three times: 'I am born under the sun sign . . . (name your sun sign). I give myself permission to shine and to reveal my . . . (list the three shining qualities of your sun sign). I am filled with pride in myself.'

TRY THIS Performing this spell on a Friday, which is ruled by the planet Venus (see page 135), can increase its potency, as can performing it when the sun is in Taurus or Libra. Consider adding a hack-proof variation of the words 'I love myself' or 'I am complete' to your online passwords. The more you see, hear and think about loving yourself, the more it will feel like your natural state.

Venus Self-Love Spell

People don't treat you as you treat them, they treat you as you treat yourself. So if you want to increase the amount of love and respect in your life, the first place to look is within. Use this charm to help you fall in love with yourself by harnessing the affectionate and loving energy of the planet Venus, which rules the sun signs Taurus and Libra.

YOU WILL NEED

- A pink or white candle
- A pen
- A piece of paper

STEPS

1 Invoke the loving energy of the planet Venus by lighting a pink or white candle and placing it securely in front of you.
2 Write on the paper three things about yourself that you are proud of. Begin each sentence with 'I love that I . . .'
3 Then, write the following affirmation three times: 'I am filled with healing love for myself. I am enough. I do not need anyone or anything else to complete me.'
4 Read out loud everything you have written.
5 Then, draw the shape of a heart in the air with your finger and kiss that imaginary heart.
6 Fold the piece of paper and place it somewhere safe, so you can read it whenever you wish.

Inner Power Visualization

Rose quartz crystal is associated with the planet Venus and is believed to have a high energetic frequency that can help boost your self-esteem and inner power. People with a sun or rising sign in Taurus or Libra will find this visualization especially therapeutic, but every sun sign can benefit from a little self-love.

YOU WILL NEED

- A rose quartz crystal

STEPS

1. Hold your rose quartz crystal in your hand and place that hand on your heart.
2. Visualize pink light and the energy of love flowing from the planet Venus into your heart until it overflows with feelings of love and peace.
3. Keep your rose quartz crystal with you at all times. Hold it in your hand and place it on your heart whenever you feel unworthy.

TRY THIS Repeat this fix for at least three weeks, which is the minimum amount of time required for rituals to make a truly positive mark on your life.

Attracting Love Rituals

Tune in to the vibration of the element that rules your sun sign to help you attract love. The elements represent creative and nurturing forces of nature which can increase your chances of love and romance.

YOU WILL NEED

- Aries, Leo and Sagittarius (Fire): items of red clothing
- Cancer, Scorpio and Pisces (Water): bubble bath or shower gel
- Taurus, Virgo and Capricorn (Earth): an indoor plant
- Gemini, Libra and Aquarius (Air): a pad of letters and envelopes

STEPS

1 **FIRE SIGN:** wear some items of red clothing or jewellery every day to attract the energy of love to you;
   WATER SIGN: transform your daily bath or shower into a ritual by visualizing the love you want to manifest in your life while you feel the water on your skin;
   EARTH SIGN: nurture an indoor plant as a symbol of the love you want to attract into your life;
   AIR SIGN: leave anonymous love notes in public spaces for unsuspecting strangers, sending out love to the world to see it come back.
2 Perform your rituals with an attitude of sacred reverence for and belief in the powerful energy of love. Repetition is key. The more often you carry them out, the more likely your chance of attracting loving people into your life.

Cancer Ritual for Better Communication

The key to happy relationships is communication. Cancerians have the ability to make others feel seen and heard. If you have a Cancer sun or rising sign, this ritual will encourage you to listen more carefully to your own inner wisdom, and to place your own needs on an equal footing with those of others. If Cancer is not your sun or rising sign, this will help you to nurture energies and boost your communication skills.

YOU WILL NEED

- A piece of paper
- A pen

STEPS

1   On a piece of paper, write down what you would like to say to someone you are having difficulties communicating with; that person could be yourself.

2   Read what you wish to say out loud. As you read, put yourself in the shoes of the person you are addressing. Are your words clear? Is there a better way to say it?

3   Tear up what you've written and use another page to rewrite what you want to say, this time expressing yourself more clearly and being conscious of the impact it will have on the listener.

4   Fold the final draft version three times, and each time you fold it say out loud: 'Miscommunication be gone. I hear you and you hear me.'

5   Carry the piece of paper with you.

TRY THIS The best time to perform this spell is when the moon is waxing, when it gives us the optimum astrological energy for letting go of what drags us down.

Pisces Forgiveness Spell

Pisces is perhaps the most forgiving sign of the zodiac. This spell encourages you to align yourself with the energy of Pisces and the planet Neptune to help you let go of feelings of hate and resentment that are dragging you down. It is designed for every sun sign, including Pisces, because although they are naturally inclined to forgive others, they can often struggle with forgiving themselves.

YOU WILL NEED
- A piece of card
- A green pen or colouring pencil

STEPS
1 Draw the shape of two fishes or circles on the piece of card using the green pen or colouring pencil.
2 In one shape write the word 'forgive' in green, and in the other write the word 'forget'.
3 Visualize your feelings of anger, resentment and hate flowing into the 'forget' shape, then colour it in so the word is crossed out and disappears. Leave the shape with the word 'forgive' as it is.
4 Then say out loud: 'I can forgive but not forget. I hate you not.'
5 Place the card somewhere you can see it every day.

Healing Heartbreak Bath

Whether you are a water sign or not, aligning yourself with the healing and nurturing energies of Cancer, Scorpio and Pisces can help to mend a broken heart.

YOU WILL NEED

- Epsom salts
- Lavender essential oil (or an oil of your choice)

STEPS

1 Spend some time reflecting on the relationship that has ended. Look at photographs or write in your diary. Allow yourself to feel all of the emotions you need to process.
2 Run a bath and add some cleansing Epsom salts and a few drops of the essential oil of your choice.
3 Step into the bath. Relax and close your eyes. Visualize the cord linking you to your ex-partner.
4 Soak in the bath, then wash yourself.
5 When you are ready, get out of the bath and collect up the rose petals.
6 As you dry yourself, watch the water drain away and visualize the cord that has been tethering you to your former partner dissolving and washing away, too.

TRY THIS Speak or think this affirmation before you make love or at the moment of orgasm when pleasuring yourself to increase the affirmation's potency.

Affirmation to Raise Your Sexual Energy

For Scorpios, sex is both a physical pleasure and a spiritually transformative experience. This simple fix will raise your vibration and help you harness Scorpio's sexual confidence, whether this is your sun sign or not. The optimum time to perform it is when the sun or moon is passing through Scorpio.

YOU WILL NEED

- Items of red, burgundy or black clothing
- A red pen
- A piece of paper

STEPS

1   During the day, be sure to wear intense and exciting colours associated with Scorpio, such as red, burgundy or black.
2   Breathe deeply, lengthening each breath until you feel harmony and a tingling sensation from your head to your toes.
3   When the sun is setting, invoke the passionate energy of Scorpio by drawing its symbol (see page 55) on a piece of paper with the red pen.
4   Below the symbol, in capital letters write the following affirmation: 'My body, mind and spirit are full of sexual energy and potential.'
5   Read your affirmation out loud three times. Memorize it.

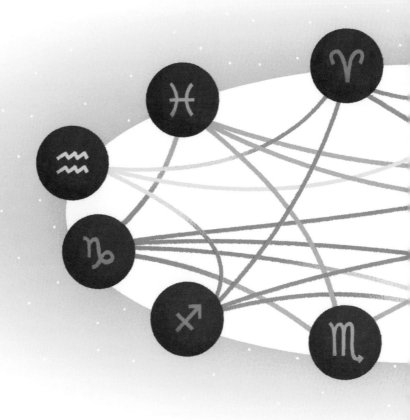

Star-Crossed Revelation

Love is the most beautiful, most mysterious energy in the world. But is our love life written in the stars? Astrology has been used for centuries as a match-making or compatibility tool. So while love is a choice you must make for yourself, you can use the stars to reflect on what might work best for you. Opposite you will find a table of compatible sun signs, but never forget that the success of any relationship is determined by what is in your heart, your desire to make the relationship work and the energy you invest in it.

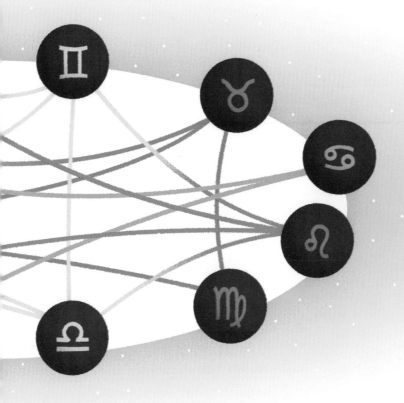

Compatible sun signs

- **ARIES:** Aquarius, Sagittarius, Leo and Gemini
- **TAURUS:** Virgo and Pisces
- **GEMINI:** Aquarius and Libra
- **CANCER:** Scorpio and Pisces
- **LEO:** Sagittarius, Libra, Gemini and Aries
- **VIRGO:** Taurus and Capricorn
- **LIBRA:** Leo and Sagittarius
- **SCORPIO:** Scorpio and Pisces
- **SAGITTARIUS:** Leo, Aries, Aquarius and Libra
- **CAPRICORN:** Pisces, Scorpio, Virgo and Taurus
- **AQUARIUS:** Gemini and Libra
- **PISCES:** Scorpio and Cancer

As a general rule, fire signs tend to get on best with other fire signs and
air signs; air signs are compatible with other air signs and fire signs. Earth signs
follow a similar pattern and mix well with each other as well as water signs;
the same applies to water signs.

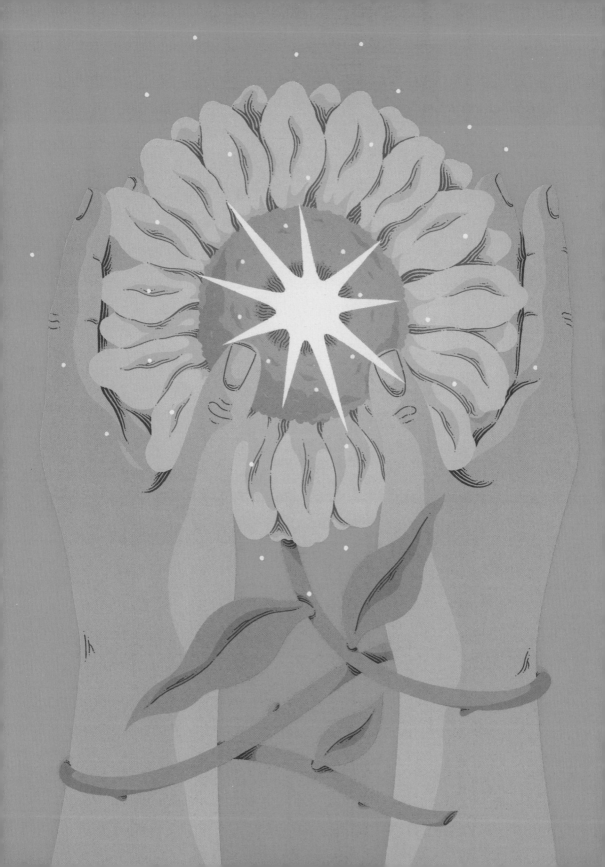

HEALTH AND WELL-BEING

The astrology fixes in this section will help you maximize and consolidate the wisdom and guidance of the stars to boost health, balance, strength, clarity and self-care

TRY THIS Use this morning mantra to focus your mind on making healthier choices.

Taurus Morning Mantra

Taurean energy can lean towards over-indulgence or comfort eating, triggering fatigue and poor health. This health-boosting mantra can be performed by everyone, regardless of their sun or rising sign and it is particularly beneficial when the sun is passing through Taurus.

YOU WILL NEED
- A mirror
- A ripe apple (preferably green, as this colour is associated with Taurus)

STEPS
1   In the morning, before you start your day, take a moment to look into a mirror.
2   Look yourself in the eye and smile. Even if you don't feel like it, fake a smile because research shows that this tricks you into feeling better.
3   Then, say out loud the following mantra: 'I want to be the healthiest and most beautiful version of myself today.'
4   Put a green apple in your bag before you set off for the day ahead and make sure you carry it with you. If you work at home, place an apple on your desk.
5   Whenever you are tempted to sample unhealthy food for comfort, take your apple out of your bag. If you do not wish to eat it, you are not hungry.
6   If you compare yourself negatively to others, remind yourself of the commitment you made, not to perfection but to be the healthiest version of yourself.

Reconnect to Earth Exercise

The earth is full of energy, and connecting with that energy can nourish and balance mind, body and spirit. Direct physical contact with the earth through 'earthing' (a healer's term for barefoot walking) has been shown to boost health. Earthing will speak most clearly to the earth signs, Taurus, Virgo and Capricorn, but it will have positive effects on all who use it and it is particularly helpful when the sun is passing through an earth sign.

YOU WILL NEED

- An area of grass, sand or mud

STEPS

1   Head outside when the weather is good and find an area of grass, sand or mud that you can safely walk on barefoot. Your garden or a local park is fine.

2   Check there are no stones or sharp objects.

3   Take your shoes and socks off and walk barefoot for a few minutes.

4   As you walk, notice how the soles of your feet feel as they make direct contact with the earth.

5   If you enjoy the natural reconnection and feel more grounded in the days that follow, let this incentivize you to try longer periods of earthing.

TRY THIS The optimum time to perform this ritual is when the sun is in Aries, Leo or Sagittarius.

Head, Heart and Hips Meditation

Each part of your body is governed by a specific sun sign. Harnessing the energy of that sign can heal or boost the well-being of that body part. This meditation will focus your concentration on the body parts associated with the fire signs: Aries, which rules the head; Leo, which rules the heart; and Sagittarius, which rules the hips and thighs.

YOU WILL NEED
- A candle

STEPS
1 Light the candle and place it securely in front of you.
2 Breathe deeply and read about the sun signs: Aries on page 28, Leo on page 36 and Sagittarius on page 44.
3 Then, close your eyes and visualize the energy and warmth of Aries flowing into your head to heal or reduce the risk of headaches, skin problems or hair loss.
4 Next, imagine the energy and strength of Leo rushing into your heart, bringing strength and healing.
5 Finally, visualize the energy and power of Sagittarius swirling around your hips and thighs and protecting you from hip and weight issues.
6 Open your eyes, touch your head, heart and hips with gratitude and blow out the candle.

TRY THIS Further improve and protect your physical and mental health with a Zodiac Detox (see page 157).

Back, Belly and Bones Exercise

This postural exercise will help to protect your back, stomach and bones by aligning you with the energies of the earth signs, Taurus, Virgo and Capricorn, which rule each of these body parts. It encourages you to focus on your posture, and how the way you stand and sit impacts your health and mood.

YOU WILL NEED
- A copy of this book

STEPS

1 Read about the earth signs: Taurus on page 31, Virgo on page 39 and Capricorn on page 47, and familiarize yourself with each of them.
2 Holding this book in your right hand, stand up straight.
3 Observe your weight distribution. Many of us tend to favour one foot over the other. Instead of slouching or leaning to one side, stand up straight with your feet parallel and about 13cm (5 inches) apart.
4 Stand tall and, while rising up, become conscious of your back and whether or not you are slumping or rolling your shoulders forward. Also reflect on the strong qualities of the bull symbol for the sign Taurus.
5 Shift your thoughts to Virgo and the attention that health-conscious sign pays to diet and exercise. Gently pull your stomach in and stand even taller than before.
6 Consider the amazing bones in your body while contemplating the practical and grounded energy of Capricorn.
7 Finally, standing as tall as possible, gently place your book on your head and hold it there for a few minutes.
8 Notice how stable and confident you feel to stand up tall, with purpose.

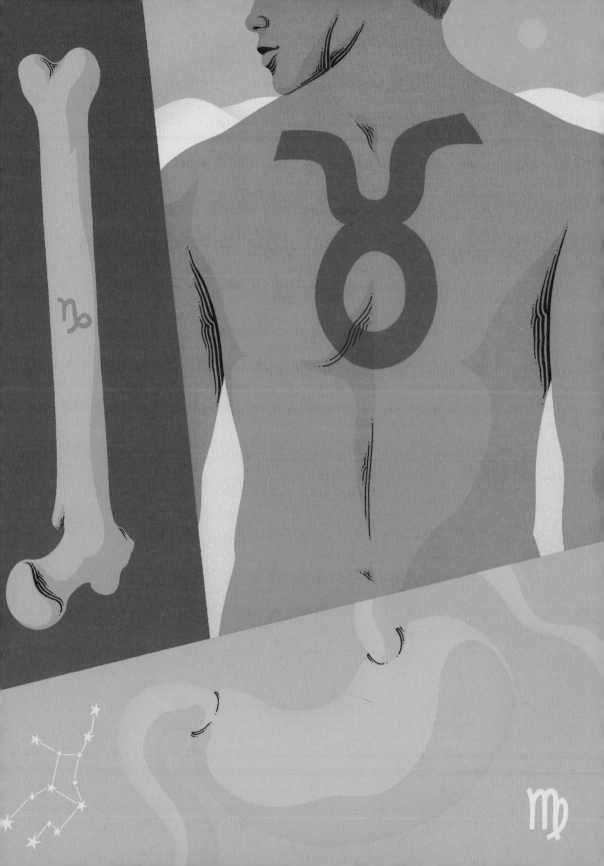

Sun-Sign Self-Care

Astrology can offer great insight into your health. Self-care – taking time to de-stress and place your own needs first – is vital for mind, body and spirit. Listed opposite are activities designed to enhance holistic health for the signs of the zodiac, and optimum ways to harness the energies of each sign. Remember that your rising sign and other planets may also play a part in your approach to your well-being.

ARIES High-energy forms of exercise, preferably outdoors, such as jogging, running and cycling, suit this sign. Punching a pillow is a great way for Arians to release pent-up tension.

GEMINI This sun sign loves team sports and cross-training, where Geminis can vary their fitness routine. The ideal way for Geminis to ease stress is by talking to friends, practising meditation or writing in a journal.

TAURUS Yoga, brisk walking and gardening appeal to Taureans. Massages and bubble baths are great stress-busters.

CANCER Indoor forms of exercise and dance suit Cancerians. Their most effective way to relax is to cook or spend time reading or with friends.

LEO Adventure sports and aerobic classes attract the lions of the zodiac. Beach holidays and taking afternoon naps are a great way for them to unwind.

VIRGO Joining a gym or working with a personal trainer suit Virgoans' organized approach to life. Decluttering is their favourite way to relax.

LIBRA Yoga and tai chi are perfect ways for Librans to exercise. Retiring early with a good book or surrounding themselves with beautiful artworks and objects can help to recharge their batteries.

SCORPIO Swimming, diving, fencing and sailing suit this sign. For Scorpios, relaxation is walking along a beach or beside a lake.

SAGITTARIUS High-energy forms of exercise and all forms of travel are ideal for Sagittarians. They love to learn and find studying a great stress-buster.

CAPRICORN Outdoor activities, walks and hikes in nature appeal to Capricorns. The best way for them to de-stress is simply to have fun doing things they enjoy.

AQUARIUS All forms of solitary exercise, such as jogging, appeal to this sign. Visiting museums and art galleries and doing volunteer work boost their mood and well-being.

PISCES Any form of fitness is beneficial to Pisceans, as they have a tendency to place a low priority on physical exercise. Meditation comes naturally to Pisceans, but they can also find massages, in particular foot massages, particularly beneficial.

> **TRY THIS** Place rose quartz close by the bath or shower, as this crystal is associated with self-love and compassion.

Go with the Flow Soak

The water signs, Cancer, Scorpio and Pisces, rule your chest, genitals and feet. This bath or shower ritual will help you direct the healing energies of these signs to the areas of the body they govern, to promote healing or boost well-being. The optimum time to perform this ritual is when the sun is in Cancer, Scorpio or Pisces.

YOU WILL NEED

- Bath oils or shower gel
- Your favourite music
- A handful of fresh herbs or flowers (rose hips and lavender are highly recommended as they ease stress and are deeply relaxing)
- Candles

STEPS

1 Read about the water signs: Cancer on page 35, Scorpio on page 43 and Pisces on page 51, and familiarize yourself with each of them.
2 Choose the sign that resonates most with you. If you have a Cancer, Scorpio or Pisces sun or rising sign, then select accordingly.
3 Set aside at least 30 minutes to turn your bath or shower into a self-care ritual and enjoy adding bath oils or gel, playing beautiful music, sprinkling in herbs or flowers and lighting candles.
4 Once you are in the bath or shower, close your eyes and focus loving thoughts on your chest, genitals or feet. Feel the energies of your chosen sign merging with the element of water and bringing healing and flow.
5 When you have washed and pampered yourself in this sacred atmosphere, get out of the bath or shower and take the relaxing energy you have soaked in with you.

TRY THIS You may want to add the symbol of
your rising sign, and even your moon sign, to this
clarity-of-mind visualization, to see what extra insight
they might bring.

Clarity of Mind Visualization

Without calm it is impossible to think clearly. This visualization draws inspiration from the stars and is designed to replace anxiety, confusion and fear with clarity, concentration and focus.

YOU WILL NEED

- A pen
- A piece of paper

STEPS

1   Draw the symbol of your sun sign (see page 55) on a piece of paper and
    write the name of that symbol underneath in capital letters. For example,
    if you are sun sign Pisces, under the symbol of two fishes swimming, write
    'two fishes'.
2   Close your eyes, slow your breathing and visualize the symbol for a few
    minutes. Focus your thoughts only on that symbol.
3   Open your eyes and brainstorm as many associations with that symbol as
    you can, however far-fetched. Write them down.
4   Then, reflect on the issue or problem causing you anxiety.
5   Without searching for an answer, review your brainstorming associations
    and see if they can bring a new perspective to your situation.

THE ASTROLOGY FIX

TRY THIS If your sun or rising sign is Gemini, Libra or Aquarius, you are soothed by the movement of the wind. If you feel stressed, you may want to indulge in a spot of kite-flying or a drive with the windows of your car down.

Connect with Air Body Scan

The air signs, Gemini, Libra and Aquarius, govern your mind, kidneys and nervous system respectively. This body scan exercise will connect you to the energies of the air signs, so you can check for anything that might be blocking the flow of energy from your mind to your body.

YOU WILL NEED
- A pen
- A notebook

STEPS

1 Draw the symbols for Gemini, Libra and Aquarius (see page 55) in a notebook and memorize them.
2 Lie down or sit on a chair.
3 Close your eyes and focus your attention first on your forehead. (You will probably notice that you are frowning without even realizing it, so gently relax your forehead and face.) Visualize the signs for Gemini, Libra and Aquarius on your forehead.
4 Next, move your mindful body scan to your neck and shoulders and gently relax them, too.
5 Turn your present attention to your arms and hands and then to your torso, before shifting your awareness to your lower body, legs and feet.
6 Check in with each body part as you go until you have noticed, without judgement, how every part of your body feels. What sensations and tensions can you detect?
7 Open your eyes. Write down what each part of your body is trying to tell you.

ENERGY AND INSPIRATION

Harness the energy of your planets and the inspiration of your
stars to bring you focus, confidence, stimulation and intuition.

Energy of Fire Boost

Feeling tired and in need of a second wind? This candle-lighting power ritual can be used by any sun sign to harness the energy-boosting power of the element of fire. Shining qualities associated with the fire signs, Aries, Leo and Sagittarius, include energy, confidence and enthusiasm.

YOU WILL NEED
- Three white candles
- Your favourite energy-boosting piece of music

STEPS
1 Find a comfortable place where you can be alone.
2 Play your favourite piece of energizing music as loud as you can.
3 Place the three candles securely in front of you.
4 Light the first candle and ask for the energy of Aries to motivate you.
5 Next, light the second candle and ask for the energy of Leo to bring you confidence.
6 Then, light the third candle and ask for the energy of Sagittarius to bring you enthusiasm.
7 Immerse yourself in the music for as long as your track plays.
8 When the track finishes, safely extinguish the candles.

TRY THIS Chant 'Om' silently in your mind, while visualizing an archer hitting their X-marks-the-spot target. This is a potent way to help your mind focus at any time.

Sagittarius Focus Mantra

The arrow symbol for the sign of Sagittarius conjures images of a hunter and the concentration and focus they have for their target. Keep your mind sharp with this attention-boosting mantra, which is particularly suited to those born with their sun or rising sign in Sagittarius.

YOU WILL NEED
- Two pencils or pens

STEPS
1 Place the two pencils or pens in the shape of an X.
2 Stare at the X shape and focus all your concentration on it.
3 Close your eyes and visualize an archer shooting their target with accuracy.
4 Open your eyes and chant 'Om' (this is pronounced Ahh-ohh-umm). 'Om' is believed to be one of the most effective mantras to help you find answers from within. The vibration of the sound represents the quiver of the arrow as it soars through the air.
5 Chant 'Om' for several minutes, or until you feel a sense of inner peace and calm.

Leo Confidence Pose

Those born with the Leo sun or rising sign are often blessed with natural charisma. This yoga pose, also known as Simhasana or Lion's Pose, is a powerful way to help every sun sign tap into the confidence of the lion, the symbol of Leo.

YOU WILL NEED
- Your voice

STEPS
1. You can perform this exercise seated, or sitting on your heels on the floor with your hands resting on your thighs.
2. Check your posture: make sure your back is straight and your shoulders relaxed.
3. Lean forward slightly, inhale deeply and open your mouth as wide as you can, with your tongue sticking out as far as it can go towards your chin.
4. With your mouth open, arch your back and exhale strongly, while at the same time roaring as loudly and as fiercely as you can: 'Haaa!'
5. Repeat two or more times, letting the lion within you roar, and feel self-doubt disappearing and your fearlessness growing.

TRY THIS Refer to pages 134–36 to learn about the associations of the planets with the days of the week, and how each day brings opportunities to invoke the energy of that planet.

Mars Action Affirmation

Mars is the planet of energy. It governs the motivation and courage of Aries and the passion and intensity of Scorpio. It also rules Tuesdays – the day of the week associated with the importance of making decisions, taking action and being stimulated (see page 135). This empowering affirmation exercise can benefit anyone, regardless of their sun sign.

YOU WILL NEED

- The day of the week to be Tuesday

STEPS

1 Every Tuesday morning, when you wake up, focus your thoughts on the energy of the planet Mars.
2 Say out loud or in your mind: 'Today the strength and energy of the planet Mars is within me. I am ready for action. I will follow my passions.'
3 Repeat the affirmation slowly three times.
4 During the day, know that the stars are in tune with your intention to take action. Seize the initiative and make decisions. Get started on projects. Do that workout. Make that call. Take action!

Mind-Wandering Meditation

Every sign of the zodiac offers an opportunity to tap in to our intuition. Fire signs are impulsive; water signs are intuitive but occasionally reserved; earth signs are cautious; and air signs are logical and clear. This mindfulness exercise encourages you to tune in to the element of air, not because it is more or less intuitive than other elements, but because traditionally air is associated with sudden and invisible insights and inspiration.

YOU WILL NEED
- A view of the clouds in the sky

STEPS

1 Set aside a few minutes to step outside. Find somewhere safe to stand or lie down.

2 Observe how the air moves things around you, from leaves on the ground to steam from rooftops, and feel the breeze on your face.

3 Now focus your attention on the clouds in the sky and their ever-changing forms. Focus all your attention on the clouds and their hypnotic, slow movements rather than any issues or problems you have.

4 Let your mind wander. When your mind is idle, areas in your brain that can creatively solve problems are triggered.

5 Spend a few minutes, or as long as you like, cloud-watching and notice if the exercise has given you a sense of seeing and feeling the air.

Age of Aquarius Reflection

Those born with their sun or rising sign in Aquarius tend to be free spirits. They take pride in their individuality and because of this have much to teach each sign of the zodiac. Just as your DNA marks your uniqueness, so too does the way you reveal the potential of the sun sign you were born into. This meditation harnesses the energy of Aquarius to inspire others to confidently walk their own path in pursuit of their dreams.

YOU WILL NEED
- A pen
- Notepaper

METHOD
1 Make yourself a cup of tea or similar hot drink.
2 Sit down somewhere comfortable and relax.
3 Closely observe the steam rising from your drink.
4 Reflect on the water-bearer symbol of the sign of Aquarius (see page 55).
5 Consider the paradox of this sign. Many think it is a water sign, but it is in fact an air sign.
6 Water symbolizes emotions, and the symbolism here is that Aquarians can carry or reflect on the emotions within themselves and in others, but not be influenced by them. This ability to distance or detach themselves from their emotions enables them to reach a better understanding of the truth.
7 As the steam releases itself from your drink, reflect on how detaching yourself from your emotions can help you make better decisions in your life.
8 Consider the possibility that, as with the symbol of Aquarius, you are not your emotions. You are simply their carrier.

TRY THIS If you don't recall any dreams on waking, repeat this ritual every evening until you do. The more often you think about having dreams, the more likely you are to remember them.

Neptune Inspiration Exercise

Every planet can be a potent source of inspiration in our lives, but there is one most often associated with unseen forces, especially the intuitive power of our dreams, and that is Neptune. The sun sign Pisces is ruled by the planet Neptune, but this ritual can help every sun sign recall their dreams and tune in to the mystical inspiration of this planet every night.

YOU WILL NEED
- A picture of the planet Neptune
- A pen
- Notepaper

METHOD
1   Imprint the image of Neptune on your mind.
2   Before you go to sleep at night, place a pen and notepaper beside your bed.
3   Close your eyes and visualize the planet Neptune out there in the infinity of deep space. As you see the image in your mind's eye, allow yourself to connect to your inner wisdom or intuition.
4   Ask Neptune to send you illuminating dreams. Tell yourself you will dream tonight and on waking you will recall your dreams.
5   Immediately on waking, write down the symbols that come to mind. The feeling of the dream is more revealing than the story, so write down how the dream made you feel, too. If you don't write your dream symbols down immediately, you will forget them.
6   Don't try to interpret your dreams straight away, but return to them later in the day to see what your intuitive wisdom is trying to tell you.

Planetary Weekday Boost

Each day of the week is associated with a specific planet. Use this fix to harness positive planet energy in your daily life from the moment you wake up. It is important to do this immediately on waking because your brain has just transitioned from a delta sleep state to a theta state. As you wake fully, you move to the more alert alpha and beta brain states, but your mind is at its most receptive to programming new ideas during the theta state.

YOU WILL NEED

- Your intention

SCHEDULE

DAY	PLANET	HARNESS ENERGY
Monday	Moon	Connect with the planet of emotions. Set intentions and find a positive mindset. Meditating and listing your goals before you start your day are highly recommended.
Tuesday	Mars	Think on the planet of action. Take steps today to set your intentions in motion. Start your day with some exercise or a brisk walk if you can.
Wednesday	Mercury	Channel Mercury the messenger. Take time to consider your preferred method of communication; do you prefer to correspond remotely or speak face to face? Do you really listen or do you find yourself focusing on your own perspective? This is the day to write in your journal, make calls and network.
Thursday	Jupiter	Connect with the planet of abundance. Focus on being optimistic and joyful. Today is a good day to expand your horizons and reflect on all that you have to be grateful for.
Friday	Venus	Speak to the planet of love. Feel encouraged to focus on your relationships. Today is the ideal day to be creative and to socialize.

Planetary Weekend Boost

Complete your week of planetary inspiration, clarity and purpose by
harnessing both Saturn and the sun's energy at the week's close. As
with the previous weekday fixes, these motivating contemplations
should be practised immediately on waking.

YOU WILL NEED
- A black pen
- A notepad
- A yellow or orange pen

SCHEDULE

DAY	PLANET	HARNESS ENERGY
Saturday	Saturn	Connect your thoughts to the planet of discipline and responsibility. Today is the day to tidy up, declutter and start planning the next week using your black pen and the notepad; black is the colour associated with Saturn.
Sunday	Sun	Now is the time to unwind and reflect calmly on whether your life is heading in the direction you want it to go. Open all of your blinds and curtains to let the sunlight in. Draw a picture of a sunflower in your notepad to remind you that a sunflower always turns towards the light. Reconnect with the creative and youthful energy of your inner child by making time for laughter today.

REST AND REJUVENATION

Use the energy of the planets and stars to relax and restore your mind and body, and bring greater awareness, motivation, harmony and calm into your daily life.

Virgo Work, Rest and Play Reflection

Practical, organized and hardworking, those born under the Virgo sun or rising sign like to get things done, and one of the reasons they are so productive is that they instinctively understand the importance of balancing their industry with regular rest. This fix is particularly beneficial for those who struggle to wind down at the end of a busy day, or for anyone who is neglecting their need for regular relaxation.

YOU WILL NEED

- A cup of your favourite tea
- A comfortable chair

METHOD

1 Make yourself a cup of tea or any other warm drink that helps you relax.
2 Find a comfortable chair to sit in.
3 Reflect on the symbol of Virgo (see page 55). What images does it conjure in your mind? Be aware that the original meaning of the word 'virgin' isn't sexual. It means 'unto yourself', or self-sufficiency and wholeness; in other words, ensuring that you are taking care of your own needs.
4 With this Virgoan inspiration in mind, slowly and mindfully drink your tea (or other beverage) and, as you do so, reflect on your life and whether you are prioritizing the needs of others over your own self-care.
5 If you aren't getting enough self-care time, make a promise aloud 'unto yourself' that you will find the essential balance between work and rest.

Learning from Yourself

During times of difficulty we have a golden opportunity to reflect on ourselves and to figure out how we can learn and grow from setbacks and failures. Sometimes it is difficult to know how to recover from disappointments, but this is where the self-awareness of astrology can help.

YOU WILL NEED
- A pen
- A notepad

METHOD
1 Reflect on a disappointment you have suffered or a mistake you have made.
2 Note down your sun sign and draw the associated symbol.
3 Write down the appropriate phrases according to your sun sign, completing the sentence in your own words..

> **ARIES:** The lesson here is . . .
>
> **TAURUS:** My strengths are . . .
>
> **GEMINI:** Next time will be better because . . .
>
> **CANCER:** Everyone makes mistakes, including me, and . . .
>
> **LEO:** I will move forward by . . .
>
> **VIRGO:** This setback is not the end because . . .
>
> **LIBRA:** I will adapt and move forward by . . .
>
> **SCORPIO:** It didn't work out but I'll try hard to . . .
>
> **SAGITTARIUS:** Success means nothing if it is easy, so next time . . .
>
> **CAPRICORN:** I can be better prepared next time because . . .
>
> **AQUARIUS:** I have learned what doesn't work, so next time . . .
>
> **PISCES:** I can forgive myself for this because . . .

4 Reflect on what the inner wisdom of your sun sign is teaching you.

TRY THIS You may find you have a lot of friends who have the same sun sign. Research that sun sign and see what life lessons are waiting there for you.

Learning from Others

It isn't just yourself that you can learn from. The people we meet in our lives are also our teachers. This astrology fix encourages you to take some time out to reflect on what the people around you are teaching you.

YOU WILL NEED
- A pen
- A notepad

METHOD

1   It is often said that we are the sum of the five people we spend the most time with. Write down the names of those people (they are not necessarily the people you love the most) and their birth dates.

2   Write down their sun signs and the following phrases beside them:

> **ARIES:** Showing a fighting spirit
> **TAURUS:** Taking time out
> **GEMINI:** Breaking the routine
> **CANCER:** Feeling at home
> **LEO:** Being adventurous and optimistic
> **VIRGO:** Practising self-care and organizing
> **LIBRA:** Seeking beauty and calm
> **SCORPIO:** Living with passionate intensity
> **SAGITTARIUS:** Worrying less, laughing more
> **CAPRICORN:** Focusing and being productive
> **AQUARIUS:** Looking ahead
> **PISCES:** Approaching things imaginatively

3   Do you feel that the five phrases (or fewer, if they have the same sun sign) resonate with you? Do you feel that the people you spend the most time with have a positive or a negative impact on you?

TRY THIS Friday is ruled by the loving and forgiving planet Venus so it is the optimum day to perform this spell, although it is potent on any weekday.

Compassion Spell

If you are angry, resentful or jealous towards someone, these feelings will prevent you from resting and recharging, because they will destroy your peace of mind. The element of water in astrology is associated with emotions, and this compassion spell can help you to release negative feelings towards others and bring you healing. It is particularly powerful when the sun is in the water signs of Cancer, Scorpio or Pisces.

YOU WILL NEED
- A glass of water
- A piece of paper
- A pencil or fountain pen

METHOD
1   Place the glass of water on a windowsill and leave it for 24 hours so it receives both sun- and moonlight.
2   After 24 hours, write the name of the person you are struggling to forgive on a piece of paper with a pencil or fountain pen.
3   Place the piece of paper in the water and leave it there until the writing becomes blurry.
4   Send that person love and healing. You may struggle to do this if they have hurt you badly, but this act of compassion is to help you release their hold over you. When you have performed this spell, notice if the relationship between yourself and the person you feel anger towards softens in the days and weeks ahead.

TRY THIS If you don't have a mirror to hand, you can draw the symbol of Jupiter with your finger onto a window pane.

Ask Jupiter Visualization

Use this astrology fix whenever you feel anxious or afraid. It will help you tap into the light-hearted, optimistic, abundant, lucky and expansive energy of the planet Jupiter.

YOU WILL NEED

- A mirror

METHOD

1 Find a mirror (preferably one that is your own) and blow onto a small area so that it steams up.
2 With your finger, draw the oddly-shaped symbol of the planet Jupiter (see page 19) in the steamed area.
3 Say out loud: 'Jupiter, bring me your light, joy and laughter.'
4 Close your eyes and visualize the energy of Jupiter flowing through you.

TRY THIS Make self-care a priority when you lose something or someone from your life. The universe always offers you an opportunity for the love you have lost to return to you and heal you.

Pluto Meditation

Pluto is the dwarf planet that governs death and endings, but also rebirth and rejuvenation. This powerful meditation will help you to cope better with loss, grief and cessation in your life, and understand that every ending offers an opportunity for a new beginning.

YOU WILL NEED

- A picture of the planet Pluto

METHOD

1 Set aside 10 minutes and find somewhere quiet where you won't be disturbed.

2 Focus your attention on the picture of Pluto for a few moments.

3 Close your eyes and focus on your breathing. Slow it down. Notice how each in-breath can't exist without an out-breath – the two are interconnected.

4 Think about the relationship or situation in your life that has come to an end. Acknowledge the pain or sorrow this is causing you. Don't try to analyze or understand it.

5 In your mind, focus on anything that you feel needs to be said or forgiven. Tell the person what you need to say. Hear what they say back to you in return. Reflect on the positive associations you have with this person. Relive these moments. Know that that they will never die or leave you.

6 When you are ready, take some slow, deep breaths and open your eyes. Carry those feelings of warmth and positivity with you and know that whoever or whatever has left your life is still alive within your heart. You can revisit them whenever you need to feel peace.

7 Close your meditation by looking at the planet Pluto again and reminding yourself that new beginnings cannot exist without endings.

Saturn Visualization

Saturn is the slowest-moving planet in the zodiac. It completes its cycle around the sun every 30 or so years. It is the symbol of maturity and lessons learned from challenges overcome and sacrifices made to progress. You may have heard the astrological term 'Saturn return' spoken with a certain degree of nervousness, as if this is going to be a period of loss and frustration. But Saturn is also the motivational and wise inner teacher or life coach.

YOU WILL NEED

- Your imagination

METHOD

1 Visualize yourself at age seven. What would this seven-year-old think about the person you are now? What piece of advice would you give your seven-year-old self?

2 Repeat this exercise for yourself aged 14, 21, 28, 35 and so on, adding seven years each time. Stop when you reach the age closest to where you are now.

3 Reflect on the wisdom you offered your past selves.

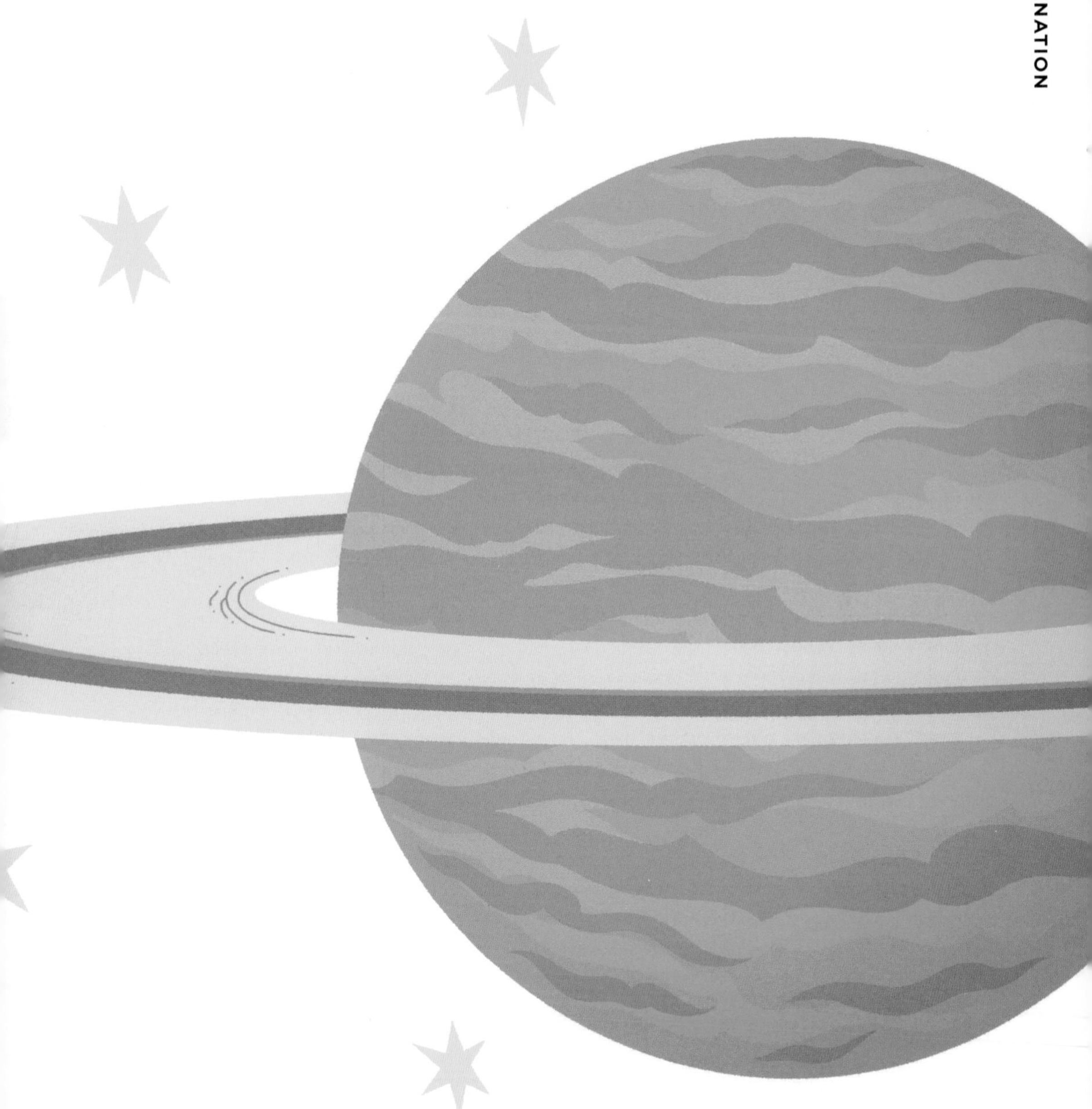

Calm Down Ritual

This simple ritual harnesses the powers of the elements to reduce stress and promote feelings of inner calm.

YOU WILL NEED

- A table or desk
- Mud or sand
- A candle
- A glass of water
- An empty glass

METHOD

1 On a small desk or table, place some mud or sand from your garden or a local park – a tiny handful will do.

2 Place a candle beside it, then a glass of water and another empty glass.

3 Light the candle safely. If you are a fire sign, say your sun sign name out loud.

4 Pick up the mud and sprinkle it into the empty glass. If you are an earth sign, say your sun sign name out loud.

5 Pour a few drops of water from the full glass onto the mud. If you are a water sign, say your sun sign name out loud.

6 Blow out the candle safely and, if you are an air sign, say your sun sign name out loud

7 Then say the following: 'With all the power and potential of my sun sign . . . (name your sun sign) and the combined cosmic forces of earth, air, fire and water, I banish stress and welcome calm into my life.'

8 Close your eyes and breathe deeply. Breathe out and imagine stress running out of you. Breathe in and imagine cosmic calm flowing into you.

TRY THIS Your rising sign presents the face you show to the world, and your sun sign your true self. Imagine your rising sign and sun sign meeting each other. What would they say to each other?

Finding Harmony Exercise

Life is about finding balance and harmony between opposites – work and rest, taking risks and following rules, endings and beginnings – and it's the same with the zodiac. There is much that we can learn from the sun sign that appears to manifest an opposite energy to our own. This astrology fix can help you find a new perspective and bring greater harmony and balance into your life by turning the spotlight on areas that you may need to develop greater strength in.

YOU WILL NEED
- A pen
- A piece of paper

METHOD
1   Write down your sun sign on a piece of paper.
2   Now note down the sun sign which is your opposite or complement:
    - Aries is opposite to Libra
    - Taurus is opposite to Scorpio
    - Gemini is opposite to Sagittarius
    - Cancer is opposite to Capricorn
    - Leo is opposite to Aquarius
    - Virgo is opposite to Pisces
3   Spend a few minutes reading about your opposite sun sign in this book (see pages 28–51).
4   Draw the symbol for your sun sign, then add the symbol for your opposite sun sign (see page 55), beside or below it so that the two symbols stand together in perfect harmony.
5   Write down the shining qualities of your opposite sun sign and reflect on ways to develop these qualities within yourself.

PROTECTION
AND COMFORT

The astrological fixes offered here are nurturing and
protective. They can be used for detoxification, security,
stability and comfort.

TRY THIS Another optimum time to detox is when the sun is passing through your opposite sign (see page 151).

Zodiac Detox

Detoxing is a great way to eliminate toxins and improve your physical, emotional and mental health. Any time is a good time to detox, but from an astrological perspective, the ideal period is when the sun is passing through the sign just before your sun sign, because this is when your cosmic energy is at its lowest. So, if you are a Cancer, the ideal time for you to detox is when the sun is passing through Gemini, and if you are a Gemini, the ideal time for you to detox is when the sun is passing through Taurus, and so on.

YOUR WILL NEED

- Your willpower

METHOD

1 Make a commitment to yourself to detox all areas of your life for one month. Detoxing doesn't have to be dramatic; it is simply limiting your exposure to foods, activities and situations that are draining you.
2 During your chosen month, drink lots of water. Watch your alcohol intake, limit the additives in your food, cut back on sugar, salt and processed foods. Focus on eating more fresh foods, wholegrains, fruit and vegetables.
3 Ensure you get a good night's sleep every night.
4 Get at least 30 minutes' exercise in the fresh air every day.
5 You may also want to switch to natural cleaning products and cosmetics.
6 Regardless of the season, declutter and spring clean.
7 Your detox month is a great time to pay attention to any negative stories you tell yourself and rewrite them.

Mercury Retrograde Remedies

Approximately three times a year, for around three weeks each time, the planet Mercury slows down and appears to move backwards (retrograde) as it passes the earth. In astrology, Mercury is the planet of communication, expression, travel and technology, and there may be an increased risk of miscommunication and mishaps when it is in retrograde. Yet this is also the ideal time to look back with the benefit of hindsight and revisit, review or renew previous commitments.

YOU WILL NEED
- Patience

METHOD
1 Find out when Mercury is next in retrograde.
2 Make 'proceed with caution' your mantra during this period and bear in mind the following considerations:
   - Pay extra care to all written communications and reread them before pressing send.
   - Pause and think before you speak.
   - Leave early when travelling to allow time for mishaps.
   - Forgive yourself and others and resolve any unfinished business with friends and acquaintances.
   - Tie up other loose ends.
   - Use your reflections on the past to inform plans for the future.

TRY THIS Whenever you are tempted to pretend to be someone you are not, or to follow and copy rather than be original, look at your picture of Uranus and remember who you are.

Uranus Meditation

Uranus is the planet of change and unpredictability, but also of freedom and innovation. This meditation will help you to align yourself with the energies of Uranus, allowing you to celebrate your uniqueness and face challenges in your life with openness and courage. It is designed for those born under the sign Aquarius, but can be used to help free the spirit of any sun sign.

YOU WILL NEED
- A candle
- A picture of the planet Uranus
- Courage

METHOD
1 Light the candle safely.
2 Visualize the picture of Uranus.
3 Say the following out loud: 'I know I am a unique miracle of DNA. There has never been and never will be another person like me. I choose to express fully my uniqueness and evolve towards the highest and best version of myself. I have confidence in myself and my future.'
4 Blow out the candle, taking a little of the courage and originality of Uranus with you.

TRY THIS Wear items of clothing and accessories in the colour that highlights the shining qualities of your sign or the sign you wish to channel. This can just be a splash of colour or subtle so long as it is worn.

Colour Fix

Research has proved the powerful impact that colour can have on our mood and well-being. Colours are carriers of energy and can boost concentration, feelings of calm and confidence. Each sun sign has a colour that it is energetically aligned with and that can bring out its shining qualities.

The next four fixes will explore the potential of colour to bring out the best of the fire, earth, air and water signs.

Fire Colour Fix: Coming Alive

ARIES

The colour for Aries is red, bringing out the energy, passion and excitement associated with this sign. Red is a traffic-stopping colour that is difficult to ignore, just as most Arians are. And don't forget that Mars – the 'red planet' rules Aries.

LEO

The colour for Leo is gold. Gold symbolizes royalty and is well-known for its association with power and authority. Leo is the king or queen of the beasts, and gold is the obvious colour to bring out the best in this confident sign, expressing as it does Leo's warmth and generosity, as well as their sunny approach to life.

SAGITTARIUS

The colour for Sagittarius is purple, which signifies opulence and abundance. Purple is also a spiritual colour, representing a visionary search for the bigger picture. It symbolizes the enlightening and expansive energy of the planet Jupiter, which rules Sagittarius.

Water Colour Fix: Feeling Good

CANCER

Cancer is associated with the colours white and silver, which is no surprise given that Cancer is fuelled by the beautiful light of the moon. White and silver are the colours of intuition and also symbolize the purity and innocence of unconditional love.

SCORPIO

Scorpio aligns with the colour black, which is fitting as Scorpio is perhaps the most intense sign of the zodiac. Ruled by forceful Mars and questioning Pluto, black symbolizes drive and the ability to see beneath the surface of things. It is also associated with death and rebirth.

PISCES

Pisces is associated with the palest green and blue, reflecting the fact that it is ruled by the planet Neptune, which is associated with the sea. These gentle, calming colours can promote healing and represent forgiveness, renewal and endless creativity.

Earth Colour Fix: Getting Practical

TAURUS

The colour for Taurus is green because green is a potent symbol of nature, growth and progress. Ruled by the planet Venus, Taurus is also a sign that symbolizes luxury and lush, new green pastures.

VIRGO

There are two colours to choose from for the sign Virgo: green and brown. Brown symbolizes the grounded nature of this sign and green represents constant growth. Ruled by Mercury, these two colours also represent the drive towards self-improvement that is characteristic of Virgo.

CAPRICORN

Capricorns, ruled by the wise planet Saturn, have two colours to choose from, both of which can accentuate their shining qualities: brown and grey. These are neutral colours and symbolize the indestructible and determined desire to achieve their goals that makes Capricorns stand out.

TRY THIS If you notice lots of shades of yellow, pink and blue in your surroundings, embrace them and let them stimulate your curiosity and inspire new ideas.

Air Colour Fix: Flying Without Wings

GEMINI

The colour for Gemini is yellow, the colour of inspiration. It has the ability to light up and breathe new life into everyone and everything. Ruled by the planet Mercury, Gemini is associated with intelligence and the power of concentration and focus to transform lives for the better.

LIBRA

Librans have two soft and beautiful colours to choose from: pink and blue. Pink is a soft and light colour and blue is a calming and cool colour. These colours bring a peaceful energy to everything they encounter, which is no surprise as Libra is ruled by the harmony-loving planet Venus.

AQUARIUS

Aquarius is aligned to the colour blue, which symbolizes the vast beauty of the skies and an easy flow of ideas and communication. Ruled by the revolutionary blue planet Uranus, Aquarius is also associated with sheer brilliance.

165

TRY THIS If you have a busy day planned, follow these steps in the morning to help prepare yourself.

Colour Visualization for Protection

Use this visualization exercise whenever you feel overwhelmed or vulnerable. Use it, too, when you feel you are losing your sense of self around others or when other people are draining your energy.

YOU WILL NEED
- Your intention

STEPS

1 When you start to feel sad, negative or vulnerable, or in need of protection, take a few deep breaths. Imagine you are breathing out stress and breathing in healing and calm.

2 Place one hand gently on your heart and the other on your stomach. These are the two places in your body where negativity can settle like an unwelcome guest. Send love and healing to your heart and gut by visualizing the coloured light of your sun sign flooding into them.

3 Then, imagine your sun sign colour circling your body like a protective bubble or an energy-catcher that not only allows joy and positivity in, but acts like a shield against negativity.

4 If you find a certain location draining, apply the same strategy. Avoid going there if you can, or physically move to a different location. If you can't do that, limit the amount of time you spend there and, when you do spend time there, visualize your protective bubble.

Conclusion
Find Your Fix

Let astrology guide and inspire your life. Whenever you need a reminder that the universe is here to help, turn to this book and meditate on the affirmations and simple solutions within. If you have a particular concern, use the 'Index by Need' (see page 174) to find the relevant fix for you. If you have any questions or insights to share, do contact me. Details of how to do so can be found on page 176.

Astrology is a remarkable tool for personal growth and transformation. Use the revealing insight it gives you about yourself, others and the journey of your life not simply to look up to but to reach for your stars.

General Index

Index by Need

Further Astrology Resources

Cheung, Theresa, *The Element Encyclopaedia of Birthdays* (HarperCollins, 2005 and 2020)
Cheung, Theresa, *The Moon Fix* (White Lion Publishing, 2020)
Faulkner, Carolyne, *The Signs: Decode the stars, reframe your life* (Penguin, 2017)
Goodman, Linda, *Sun Signs* (Pan Books, 1999)
(Other recommended titles by Linda Goodman include *Love Signs* and *Star Signs*)
Greene, Liz, *Astrology for Lovers* (Conari Press, 2008)
www.asktheastrologers.com – *free rising-sign calculator*
http://astrostyle.com/free-chart/ – *free birth chart*
http://www.lunarium.co.uk/moonsign/calcualtor.jsp – *free moon-sign calculator*
https://www.timeanddate.com/moon/phases/– *schedule for the next full moon*
www.moonology.com
www.astro.com

Also available

The Moon Fix
by Theresa Cheung

The Crystal Fix
by Juliet Thornbury

The Flower Fix
by Anna Potter

Acknowledgements

Sincere gratitude to my editor, Zara Anvari, for being the guiding force behind this book and to Charlotte Frost for her invaluable help with final editing. I'd also like to thank everyone at Quarto involved in the illustrations, publication and promotion of this book.

Thank you to my wise agent Jane Graham Maw (www.grahammawchristie. com) and also to Ingrid Court-Jones for her amazing help with early copy-editing of my material. And last, but by no means least, deepest love and gratitude to Ray, Robert and Ruthie, as I immersed myself in the blissful ritual of writing this book by day and, of course, by starlight.

About the Author

Theresa Cheung has her sun sign in Aries, her rising sign in Virgo and her moon sign in Cancer. She was born into a family of astrologers and psychics. Since leaving King's College, Cambridge, she has written numerous bestselling mind, body, spirit books and encyclopaedias, including two *Sunday Times* Top-10 bestsellers. She has sold well over half a million books and her titles have been translated into more than 30 languages and have become international bestsellers. She has written features about personal growth and spiritual development for magazines and national newspapers, and her radio and TV work include an interview about spirituality with Piers Morgan on GMTV and an appearance on Russell Brand's *Under the Skin*. She works closely with scientists studying consciousness and dreams, and is collaborating with The Institute of Noetic Sciences (IONS). Theresa's website is www.theresacheung.com.

Get in Touch

To contact Theresa, feel free to reach out to her via her Facebook and Instagram author pages. You can also email her via her website or direct at angeltalk710@aol.com. Theresa endeavours to reply to everyone who messages her. However, please bear in mind that sometimes it can take her a while to reply when life gets super busy – or if it's a starry night!